Other Books by Melissa Donovan

ADVENTURES IN WRITING (SERIES)

101 Creative Writing Exercises
10 Core Practices for Better Writing
1200 Creative Writing Prompts

Get all three books in one volume: *Adventures in Writing: The Complete Collection.*

THE STORYTELLER'S TOOLBOX (SERIES)

What's the Story? Building Blocks for Fiction Writing
Story Drills: Fiction Writing Exercises

NOVELS

Engineered Underground (Metamorphosis Book One)

Melissa also writes children's books under the pen name Emmy Donovan.

The Storyteller's Toolbox

Story Drills:
Fiction Writing Exercises

Melissa Donovan

Swan Hatch Press | San Francisco

The Storyteller's Toolbox
Story Drills: Fiction Writing Exercises

First Edition, 2018
Published by Swan Hatch Press • Melissa Donovan

ISBN 10: 0-9976713-1-9
ISBN 13: 978-0-9976713-1-5

Library of Congress Control Number: 2018904871

The Storyteller's Toolbox

Story Drills:
Fiction Writing Exercises

Table of Contents

Introduction

Learning any craft requires study, practice, and introspection. The craft of storytelling requires a whole lot more.

Many people think stories come pouring out of authors, words flowing, characters fully formed, and plots totally developed. But the truth is that telling stories is hard work.

A story—especially a novel-length story—is composed of many different building blocks: characters, plot, setting, theme, chapters, scenes, action, dialogue, exposition—not to mention point of view, tense, style, tone, and voice. There's more, but you get the idea: stories are complex, and writing good stories requires a wide range of skills.

We need to understand what makes characters tick. We need to engineer intriguing plots and develop meaningful themes. And we need to structure our stories to be interesting, to keep readers turning pages. We need to choose the best possible narrative. And then there's grammar, spelling, and punctuation. A story has a lot of moving parts, and they all need to be in sync for the story to flow smoothly.

Everything matters in storytelling. There's a lot to learn, and once we learn the basics, we need practice—lots and lots of practice—before we can hope to truly master the craft.

What You'll Find Inside This Book

This book takes you through the core elements of storytelling, including characterization, plot, setting, and theme, and then it guides you through story structure and narrative writing. You'll explore literary devices and narrative techniques, and you'll experiment with methods that will help you develop your best writing process. Finally, you'll learn how to deconstruct stories and study them to strengthen and improve your own work.

Each exercise in *Story Drills* includes a comprehensive description of a storytelling concept followed by three exercises. The "Study" exercises show you how to examine stories to better understand each concept; "Practice" exercises prompt you to apply the concepts to your own work; and "Questions" offer inquiries for further contemplation and deeper understanding of storytelling concepts and techniques.

Story Drills also includes an appendix packed with worksheets that you can use to plan and develop stories of your own.

How to Use This Book

When we need to write but find ourselves at a loss for words, writing exercises can inspire us. Exercises can also help us keep our writing muscles in shape when we're between projects. But most importantly, fiction writing exercises impart useful tools and techniques that will strengthen our storytelling skills.

There's no right or wrong way to use this book. If you're struggling with a story and need help with a particular problem, jump to the section of the book that addresses it. If you're feeling uninspired and need a little motivation, open to any random page. If you want to sharpen all your storytelling skills, work your way through *Story Drills* from beginning to end.

Story Drills is designed to be used by individual writers or in the classroom. It includes over a hundred fiction writing exercises that build storytelling skills, taking aspiring storytellers through the most important elements and steps of crafting a story.

To learn more about the Storyteller's Toolbox—a series of books on the craft of writing fiction—visit writingforward.com.

Part I:
Characters

1

Characters with Purpose

Each character in a story needs a purpose, a function they fulfill that is necessary. For example, the antagonist's purpose is to provide obstacles and challenges for the protagonist. Many protagonists find themselves under the tutelage of a mentor; the mentor's purpose is to impart skills, gifts, or wisdom that the protagonist will need as the plot unfolds.

Not every character gets a high purpose—some function as props or part of the setting—a bartender, a taxi driver, and a host of other characters that are usually unnamed often appear in only one scene and have no real bearing on the story.

However, most named characters play a vital role in a story, and this role may not be clear to readers until they reach the story's end. Throughout most of *The Wonderful Wizard of Oz*, we believe the Wizard of Oz is a great magician with the power to grant Dorothy's wish to return home to Kansas. It's not until the story nears its ending that we realize the Wizard of Oz is a fraud. He can't grant Dorothy's wish because he's not a magician. His function in the story is to act as a foil or a trickster, a character that misleads other characters.

Characters that lack purpose can cause a story to feel weak or watered down. Multiple characters who share a single purpose can also weaken a story. One strong, vital character will enrich a story more than two weak, vague characters that work together to perform a single function.

Usually we can determine a character's purpose by analyzing their relationship to the protagonist and examining how they assist or impede the protagonist or how they move the plot forward. A good test of a character's purpose is to think about how the story would be affected if the character were removed.

Study:

Choose a story that you know well, make a list of the ten most important characters in the story, and note each character's purpose to the story.

Practice:

We'll start with a protagonist—a city detective working on a burglary case. The antagonist is an FBI agent working on a federal drug bust. Their paths collide because the house that was burglarized is connected to the drug bust. Develop five supporting characters within this story, writing a sentence or two about each one's purpose to the story. As an alternative, feel free to come up with your own story premise: create a protagonist, an antagonist, and five supporting characters with clearly defined purposes.

Questions:

Can you think of any stories that include unnecessary characters with no essential purpose? If they were removed, how would the story change? Would removing them have made the story better?

2

Character Arcs

In storytelling, an arc is a path of transformation. A character arc is the journey that a character experiences throughout the course of a story, which leads to a significant change.

Changes can occur internally or externally. Characters can acquire or lose knowledge, skills, or emotional strength—or they can gain or lose relationships, material possessions, or status. Some of the best character arcs are a combination of both internal and external transformations.

A character's arc can be positive or negative. Most heroes emerge from a story wiser, stronger, or better off in some significant way. However, some characters experience a downward spiral—they are on top of the world when we meet them, and then we watch them fall. A character's arc can also wind through the story's events—up and down—only to lead back to where they were at the beginning.

An arc is common—some say essential—for a protagonist, but any character in a story can experience an arc. In *Star Wars: Episode IV A New Hope*, the protagonist, Luke Skywalker, undergoes significant growth, but supporting character Han Solo also gets a meaningful arc that is critical to the story.

At its core, an arc signifies transformation and gives the events of the story deeper meaning—after all, stories are about conflict, and what good is conflict if it doesn't produce meaningful change in our lives?

These changes range from deeply significant to superficial. Some characters will start out as store clerks and end up as store managers. Others will save the world.

Character arcs don't appear in all stories. Stories with minor or nonexistent character arcs are usually plot driven. For example, police procedural series tend to focus more on showing the detective solving crimes in each installment without undergoing much meaningful personal transformation.

There are some common milestones that characters experience throughout an arc, especially the protagonist; these include establishing goals or realizing that they want or need something; facing conflicts and challenges; making difficult decisions; and experiencing the consequences of their decisions (good and bad). As a result of these experiences, the characters are transformed by the end of the story.

Study:

Choose a character from a story you know well and plot the character's arc, noting the choices the character makes as well as the gains, losses, and transformations that the character experiences. Make sure you note the corresponding story event with the change that it effects in the character.

Practice:

Start with the following premise: A child's mother dies while the father is overseas on a top-secret mission. The child is put in foster care for almost a year until the father returns. Make a list of five plot points and describe how each one changes the protagonist. Then write a paragraph describing the protagonist's arc over the course of the story. Feel free to come up with your own story premise for this exercise.

Questions:

Can you think of any protagonists that don't change over the course of a story? Can you think of some supporting characters who experienced significant arcs? How does a character arc enrich the reader's experience?

3

Protagonist vs. Antagonist

We often think of them as the good guy and the bad guy or the hero and the villain, but those terms are misleading. A story's protagonist is the focal character—the character whom the story is about. Protagonists usually have a goal, encounter serious challenges, make difficult choices, face consequences, and undergo meaningful transformation. Protagonists aren't always benevolent. The anti-hero is an example of a protagonist that doesn't embody the classic traits of a hero, such as strength, morality, or courage.

A common misconception is that an antagonist is a villain. Villains are almost always antagonists, but not all antagonists are villains. The antagonist is essentially an obstacle that prevents the protagonist from achieving their goals. For example, if the protagonist and his best friend are vying for the quarterback position on the football team, the best friend will be the antagonist but not a villain.

The antagonist and protagonist can also be embodied in a single character, which occurs when the only thing standing in the protagonist's way…is the protagonist.

The antagonist isn't always a character. In a story about a natural disaster, the antagonist could be a hurricane, a tornado, or an asteroid hurtling toward Earth. Most of these stories also include human antagonists that provide a source of conflict and drama, but a storm alone can function as a story's sole antagonist.

Study:

Make a list of ten books, movies, and TV shows. If you're feeling up to it, make a list of up to twenty-five. For each story, jot down the protagonist and the antagonist.

Practice:

Sketch three sets of protagonists and antagonists, writing a one-paragraph description of each. Remember, these two characters have a fundamental conflict with each other. What is it? Make your first pair a traditional hero and villain. Make one of your pairs friends or family members. For the third pair, create a nonhuman antagonist. For extra practice, summarize a story premise where the protagonist is also the antagonist.

Questions:

Have you ever encountered a protagonist who wouldn't be considered a hero? What about an antagonist that wasn't a villain? Why is the conflict between a protagonist and an antagonist so important in storytelling? Do you think it's possible to tell a story without a protagonist or antagonist?

4

Archetypal Characters

There are dozens of character archetypes that populate the universe of storytelling. Each archetype has a core function to perform in the story they inhabit. Today, we'll look at eight common archetypes, all of which are found in the Monomyth (Hero's Journey), which was discovered by Joseph Campbell. Here's a brief overview:

Hero: The central figure of a story who embarks on a journey, which results in personal transformation (and usually transformation of the world as well).

Herald: A character that signals change. The Herald often appears near the beginning of a story and marks the commencement of the Hero's Journey. In *Alice in Wonderland*, it's the White Rabbit.

Mentor: The Mentor bestows wisdom, skills, or essential gifts to the Hero.

Threshold Guardian: The Threshold Guardian's job is to try to block the Hero from getting from one point in the story to another. Threshold Guardians are often aligned with the antagonist, but they can also be allies of the Hero.

Shapeshifter: The Shapeshifter causes confusion and uncertainty, often through lies and other duplicitous behavior, but the Shapeshifter doesn't have to be an antagonist and may be one of the Hero's allies.

Shadow: The Shadow is often a story's villain or

antagonist, but Shadows can also manifest in other types of characters. The Shadow embodies the inverse of the Hero's best traits: if a Hero's best trait is their loyalty, the Shadow will be treacherous.

Trickster: Tricksters provide mischief and comedic relief, and they often act as a stand-in for the audience, asking obvious questions, like "Why are we walking into a tunnel if we think there's a dragon at the other end?"

Allies: Friends of the protagonist, Allies are helpers who provide various forms of assistance to the protagonist throughout the course of the story.

Characters can embody more than one archetype within a single story. An Ally can also be a Trickster or a Shapeshifter. The Mentor can be a Threshold Guardian.

Study:

Make a list of the eight archetypes above. Drawing from any stories, list three characters that represent each archetype.

Practice:

Create a cast of characters based on the eight archetypes above. Start by stating the Hero's main objective in a story (for example, finding a hidden treasure). Build the cast by writing a few sentences about each archetypal character. You may find that you've got a rough outline for a story when you're done!

Questions:

Are any of these archetypes necessary to all stories? Which archetype do you think is the most expendable? Does each archetype have an obvious purpose? Can you think of any other archetypes that have built-in purpose to a story? What is the difference between an archetypal character and a stereotypical or stock character?

5

Getting out of Your Comfort Zone

Have you ever read a story in which the characters were so similar to one other that you became confused as to which character was speaking or acting in any given scene? Or worse, have you read a story where the characters were so dull or similar to one another that they bored you?

The luckiest storytellers have a lot of worldly experience. They've known people from many walks of life and can depict a variety of personalities in their fiction. But most of us have a relatively limited experience with the world at large. Maybe you've never lived in a rural area. Maybe you've never known someone from another country. Maybe all your friends and family are of the same political or religious persuasion. Maybe your story requires a police officer, an accountant, or a scientist, but you've never met or known any such people. Maybe your story includes people whose race, religion, or gender is different from yours.

There are a few ways to acquire the skills necessary to depict characters that are different from you: read books by and about different types of people, watch documentaries, conduct interviews, use beta readers who can expertly check your depictions. Most of all: get out of your comfort zone.

Study:

Make a list of three traits or qualities that you do not possess and have not experienced personally. These can range from living on a farm to having a hot temper to a different ancestry. Make sure these traits also do not belong to anyone that you know personally. In other words, if you've never met an astrophysicist, an astrophysicist can go on your list. Next find some material that will help you glean understanding of traits and qualities you've selected. The internet is an ideal resource for this—you can read articles or short stories and watch videos in just a few minutes. You can even find and follow people who embody the traits you're researching on social media. The goal is to gain some understanding of someone who is different from you.

Practice:

Write a short personal essay from the perspective of someone who is your polar opposite.

If you've lived in a small town all your life, write about an army brat who was raised living in dozens of cities, going to different schools each year. Are you a stay-at-home parent living in the suburbs? Write as a swinging single making it big in the big city. If you're a successful businessperson from a privileged background, write as a prison inmate. If you're a Buddhist, write from the perspective of a Christian. If you're Christian, write from the perspective of an atheist. Are you a political junkie? Write from the viewpoint of the political ideology you oppose.

For the essay, focus on something you have never experienced or that you disagree with. If you're from the city and you're writing about the country, write a descriptive essay about a farm setting. If you're a liberal writing as a conservative, choose an issue and write an essay arguing for the conservative position on that issue.

The idea is to get out of your comfort zone and explore a different way of life or mode of thinking than the one you know and have experienced firsthand. You can then use this exercise to develop a character who is truly different from you.

When you're done, find someone with the expertise to read your essay and give you honest and critical feedback about whether you captured the essence of the character you were trying to represent.

Questions:

How much of our own life experience, personality, and behavior do we bring into the characters we create? Do we tend to create characters that are similar to ourselves, or do we create characters who are totally different from us? How can we create a cast of characters that stand out from each other? And how can we accurately depict people whose life experience, viewpoints, and personalities are different from our own while still depicting them in a way that is authentic?

6

Internal and External Struggles

In order to develop a truly compelling character, it's critical for an author to know what the character wants and what's standing in the character's way.

If you want to create a complex character, identify an external goal and an internal struggle for the character, and make sure the goal and struggle are at odds with each other. For example, in *The Hunger Games*, Katniss Everdeen struggles internally because she doesn't want to hurt anyone; however, to survive the Hunger Games, she needs to kill her opponents—survival is her external goal. This pits her personal values (don't harm others) against her external goal (survive).

When a story demands that a character challenge or reevaluate their internal goals and values, things get interesting. This is a surefire recipe for some much-needed conflict.

Another strategy for developing internal and external conflict is figuring out what a character wants and what a character needs. When a character's wants and needs clash, conflict arises naturally, and the character becomes infinitely more interesting.

Study:

Choose three protagonists from books, movies, or TV shows and identify an external goal and an internal struggle for each one. Then write a paragraph about how the external goal and internal struggle are in conflict with each other.

Practice:

For this exercise, create a new character with an external goal and an internal struggle that are in conflict with each other. Make sure you describe what's at stake for this character.

Questions:

How often are our values or personal goals challenged in real life as compared to in fictional stories? How do stakes and consequences factor into the decisions that characters make when choosing between goals and morals? Can you explain, in your own words, why the conflict between a character's external goals and internal values is interesting and useful in a story?

7

Character Backstory

Backstory is everything that happened to the characters or in the story world before the narrative begins. You could say that fiction is built on backstory. In fact, many authors spend countless hours developing backstory, most of which never makes it into the final narrative. However, the author's knowledge of the story's history bleeds into the prose, enriching it with realism.

In some cases, knowledge of backstory is essential in order for the story to make sense. In the film *Titanic*, it's important for us to learn that Rose's father lost the family fortune and died, leaving Rose and her mother penniless. Without that knowledge, the audience will wonder why it's so critical for Rose to marry the wealthy aristocrat Cal.

Backstory can be revealed in various ways. Some stories use flashbacks, fully fleshed-out scenes that took place in the past. Others reveal backstory through dialogue and exposition.

Some even use information dumps. A good rule of thumb is to avoid including too much backstory in a manuscript unless it's necessary to understanding the narrative.

Character backstory is useful for creating realistic and believable characters. Everyone has a past—characters should too. By the time we encounter them, most characters have lived long enough to have formidable personal histories.

To gain a deeper understanding of your characters, you can step outside of your story and spend some time developing backstories for them. It helps to start at the beginning:

> *Sarah James was born in a small town south of San Francisco just a few days before the 1906 Earthquake. Her mother was a schoolteacher, and her father ran a general store...*

A character backstory can be simple, covering the highlights and significant events of your character's life. Backstory can also be elaborate and delve into a lot of detail. Character backstory is useful when it's peppered with details that are linked to the character's situation within the story. For example, a character who lives and works in a big city and who's jumpy and uncomfortable with all the big-city noises might be explained as having spent the first thirty years of her life living in a quiet rural area.

Study:

Choose a character from a book, TV show, or movie. List everything you know about the character that happened prior to the narrative's beginning. Make notes about how this information was revealed (flashbacks, dialogue, exposition, etc.).

Practice:

Create a new character. Write about two pages or five hundred words of the character's backstory starting with your character's birth and hitting all the major events of your character's life up to the point when the story starts. Try to include a mix of positive and negative experiences; show the character's interests, goals, strengths, and weaknesses; and be sure to include the character's relationships with other people.

Questions:

Why is it helpful for authors to develop character backstories if most of that information will never appear in the narrative? Can you think of any characters that had no backstories? What about characters that had rich, elaborate backstories? What positive or negative impact does character backstory have on the narrative?

8

Character Choices

We get to wherever we are in life through circumstance and the choices we make. Sometimes we make good decisions. Sometimes we make bad decisions. Sometimes our decisions are neither good nor bad but a matter of personal preference. Decisions run the gamut from minor issues, like how we deal with spilling coffee on a new shirt, to major issues, like deciding whether to have a child or get a divorce.

The choices we make say a lot about who we are. They reveal our tastes, interests, priorities, and moral codes.

The same is true for characters and the choices they make. If you want to see what kind of people your characters are, force them to make difficult decisions, and their inner workings will be revealed. Such choices are integral to characterization and conflict and therefore are almost always present in stories.

Study:

Think of situations from stories in which a character had to make a difficult or meaningful decision. Write a description of the situation, the choices that were available to the character, the choice the character ultimately made, why they made that choice, the consequence of that choice, and what their decision says about the kind of person they are.

Practice:

Use a character from a story you're writing, or quickly sketch a new character for this exercise. Put the character in a situation that forces the character to make a difficult decision. There should be at least three options for the character to choose from. Now write three different scenes, each showing the character in the same situation but making a different decision in each scene. The narrative should explain why the character makes a particular choice and what the consequences will be.

When you're done writing your three scenes, write one sentence for each scene summarizing what the choice says about the character. Does making a different choice fundamentally change the character's personality?

Questions:

How do the choices that characters make create conflict? How do their choices resolve conflict? What can a character's decisions reveal about the character? As an author, how do you decide which choices your characters will make? Are they based on the character or the plot?

9

Building a Cast

Casts are all about relationships, and relationships are complex. Some characters have a strong bond; others don't get along. Some work together; others sleep together. Some characters are trying to achieve a goal while others work to prevent them from succeeding.

We think of stories as being focused on a protagonist, but it's often the strength of the cast that makes a story dynamic. Take *Star Wars: Episode IV A New Hope* for example. Luke Skywalker was the hero of the film. He was (and is) beloved, but many of the secondary and tertiary characters enjoyed more popularity with audiences.

Characters that complement but contrast each other tend to work best in a cast. If the characters share goals, values, or lifestyles, they need traits that distinguish them from one another, like skills, personalities, behaviors, or backgrounds. A balance of conflict and harmony offers ample opportunity for interpersonal drama, suspense, and of course, tension.

Effective casts are fraught with friction of all kinds: friends get in fights, lovers make up, enemies meet on the battlefield—and all of this happens as the central plot hurtles toward its climax and conclusion.

Study:

Choose a book, movie, or TV show with a cast of at least five primary characters. Diagram the relationships between the characters showing working relationships, friendships, familial relationships, and romances as well as antagonistic relationships. If relationships change over the course of the story, include notes about those changes and how they come about. List one to three key personality traits for each character so you can easily see how the personalities contrast with each other. Jot down what the characters share in common or what bonds them as well as sources of friction between them.

Practice:

Develop a cast of five or more characters for a story. Don't worry about plot; focus on creating characters that complement and contrast one another to build a cast with interesting dynamics. Some ideas to get you started: a family, students, coworkers, passengers on an airplane, people who've gotten stuck in an elevator. Write a short paragraph of description for each character, and then diagram the cast, showing their relationships, personalities, commonalities, and differences.

Questions:

Which members of a cast get along with each other? Which are always at odds? What do they share in common? What are their differences? Do the characters break off into smaller groups or partnerships? How do the relationships between the characters change over time?

10

Character Chat

Most of us have used online chats or text messaging, but how many of us have held up both sides of the conversation?

Have you ever thought about having conversations with your characters?

Conversations can be revealing, exposing a person's interests, values, attitudes, and other personality traits. Sometimes through conversation you learn someone's history, their problems, or their passions. This can work with characters too.

You're going to do a little playacting, which involves playing yourself and your character. You'll do it through a mock chat.

Before you start, you might want to come up with a list of questions to ask your character. Also, this is a great exercise to use when you get stuck in a story that doesn't want to move forward. Simply chat with your character to try to find out what's holding them back from taking the next step.

Study:

Find an online forum or chatroom (search for "chatroom transcripts"), and then observe a few conversations. Take notes about what each person's postings reveal about them.

Practice:

Launch your word processing software and start a conversation with your character. Your chat might look something like this:

Writer: You're just sitting there, doing nothing. What's your problem?

Character: I don't know what to do.

Writer: What are your options?

Character: I have no options. You've written me into a corner, and there's no way out.

Questions:

If you could talk to your characters, what would you say to them? What would they say to you? Is there anything about your characters that you don't know or understand? What would you want your characters to reveal to you, the author, and what should they reveal to the readers?

11

Voice Monologue

According to Merriam-Webster's, a monologue is "a dramatic sketch performed by one actor" or "a literary composition written in the form of a soliloquy." Basically, it's when one person talks nonstop, usually to an audience.

Monologues often reveal interesting things about the speaker; among these are the speaker's voice—the way they string words together.

Think about your friends, family members, and coworkers. They frequently use certain words and phrases. There are idiosyncrasies in the way they talk—sometimes pronouncing a word in an unusual way. Some people speak with simple language; others have a vast vocabulary.

In fiction, characters will be more realistic if each has a unique voice—their own distinct way of speaking.

Study:

Read or watch at least five monologues to gain understanding of how they flow, how they're structured, and how they work within a larger story. Hamlet's soliloquy "To Be or Not to Be" is one of the most famous monologues in English literature. You can also find good monologues in films like *A Few Good Men* or *Pulp Fiction*. You can do an online search for monologues in plays (which you can read) or films (which you can watch). Don't forget to take notes!

Practice:

Write a monologue in first person from your character's perspective. Choose a general theme for the monologue, and then write the monologue with the intent to discover or develop the character's voice. The topic isn't as important as finding the character's voice, but here are some ideas to help you get started:

- The character is relating a significant event from their past: the loss of a loved one, a major life transition, or one of those everyday moments that change everything or stay with you forever.

- The character is faced with a serious challenge or decision and is discussing the options and the possible consequences of their choices.

- The character is in the middle of an emotional crisis and is overcome by grief, rage, envy, or some other intense feelings.

- The character is giving a speech or lecture on a topic that they are knowledgeable about.

Include an introductory paragraph establishing the situation in which the character is giving a monologue, including which other characters are there to witness it. The monologue should be a minimum of 750 words. Revise and polish it until you get the character's voice just right.

If you're feeling really brave (or if you're an actor at heart), try recording yourself reading or acting out the monologue. That will add another dimension to the character and allow your character's speech, intonation, and inflection to come through as well as their physical behaviors and mannerisms.

Questions:

In what situations would a character give a monologue? What can the audience learn from a monologue that can't be learned through action or dialogue? Can you think of any monologues you've read or watched that you thought were particularly effective? Which is your favorite and why?

12

Unmasking

Who doesn't love a good surprise? Audiences appreciate a surprise ending, especially if they're unable to see the twist coming. But surprises don't have to come at the end of a story. Some of the best stories are peppered with delightful surprises that prompt readers to keep turning the pages.

But be careful—poorly executed surprises and twists can come off as cheap ploys, unbelievable or obvious, or contrived. The best surprises feel natural. Readers will say, "I didn't see that coming, but now it totally makes sense!"

Surprises usually occur in the story's plot, but surprises that change our view of a character are also enticing. When the characters are full of surprises, they take on new dimensions, and as the characters' secrets are revealed and their true selves are unmasked, readers will be thrilled by the surprise—if it's executed well.

For this exercise, be careful not to confuse a character's transformation with a surprise unmasking. When a character changes, they start out one way and become different as a result of their experiences. In an unmasking, we learn that the character wasn't who we thought they were all along.

Study:

A few movies that delivered characters unmasking include *Primal Fear*, *The Usual Suspects*, and *The Jane Austen Book Club*. Books that offer characters unmasking include *Gone Girl* or A Song of Ice and Fire (series). All of these books and movies are worth reading and watching and will get you thinking about characters in new ways.

Find a character in a story that gets unmasked and write a one-page essay (about 250 words) describing who you thought the character was, how the truth about the character was revealed, who the character really was, and why it matters to the story.

Practice:

Develop a character that will be unmasked during a story. It can be a primary character like the protagonist, or it can be a secondary character. The character can be good or bad or somewhere in between. The unmasking can be a simple secret the character keeps that changes our entire perception of the character when it's revealed, or the character can be a shapeshifter—presenting as something quite different from what they truly are. Avoid obvious and traditional shapeshifters like vampires and werewolves for this exercise; try to come up with something fresh.

Questions:

What happens when the character we thought was a hero's ally turns out to be working for the villain? Why are surprises like these so enticing to readers? How can unmasking a character enrich a story? Should a story include clues, like foreshadowing, that provide hints about the character's true nature? Why would this be beneficial?

13

Character Sketch

A character sketch isn't a drawing or an illustration. It's a detailed description of a character, often written as a list of traits, plus some prose describing the character's backstory.

Character sketches serve several purposes that are useful to authors. Sketches help authors get to know their characters before bringing them into a story's action. We know what they look like, what they want, and what kind of decisions they would make. This can make the writing of a first draft flow smoothly because we don't have to stop every few pages and wonder what the character would do or what they're thinking.

Sketches can also help us figure out whether members of a cast will work well together. You can work out relationships and conflicts between characters based on the personalities you've established for them, and you can fix problems before writing the story, eliminating the need for future revisions.

Some authors sketch all major characters before starting a draft. Others only make notes of the most important or relevant character traits, especially those that will be necessary to the story. Character sketches can be updated as a story progresses. They're especially useful for authors who are writing series. Many series writers keep a story bible that they can refer to later; character sketches help them keep track of details about the characters that they might forget by the time they get to the fifth or sixth book in a series. Sketches are also useful when writing massive, complex stories with a lot of characters.

You can include as much or as little detail as you want in a character sketch. Maybe you don't need physical descriptions of your characters, but you want to figure out their backstories so they feel more realistic. Maybe instead of writing physical descriptions, you prefer to use photos. Maybe you only need to sketch your primary characters, and you'll let your secondary characters surprise you when they show up in the story.

The character sketch is a tool for authors and should be used in whatever way best helps your storytelling process.

Study:

Choose a character from a of your favorite story. Use the character-sketch template in the appendix to describe the character; include as much detail as you can.

Practice:

Create a new character using the character-sketch template that is provided in the appendix.

Questions:

What are the benefits of creating character sketches before writing a story? Can you think of any drawbacks? Why might you start with a vague character sketch and then fill in the details as you develop your story's outline or write a first draft?

14

Character Diaries

Sometimes a character remains vague, elusive, or distant, even after you've completed a character sketch and drafted the character's backstory. One way to bring clarity to a character is to get inside the character's head.

Writing a diary from a character's perspective is an exercise in finding out what's in your character's heart and mind. The intimate nature of a diary can reveal the character's thoughts, feelings, attitude, goals, fears, and more.

Character diaries are useful if you're writing a third-person narrative and want to get some insight into what any particular character is thinking or feeling. They're just as useful when you're developing a first-person narrative and want to explore the narrator or any of the other characters in your story.

The character diary becomes exploratory material that won't be included in the narrative but provides valuable information about a character that will shape and inform the character's actions within the narrative. Think of it as research.

When writing character diaries, relax and take a few moments to crawl inside your character's skin. What does it feel like to be this character? What does the world look like from this character's perspective?

Study:

Choose a character from a story you've read recently, and write three short diary entries from the character's perspective. Each entry should be at least two hundred words. Write in the character's voice and articulate the character's thoughts and feelings in a way that might not have been stated outright in the story.

Practice:

Write five diary entries from one of your characters' perspectives. You can create a new character for this exercise—feel free to use the character sketch in the appendix to develop a new character. Each entry should be at least 250 words. Write in the character's voice, and explore the character's innermost thoughts and feelings.

Questions:

How does your mindset change when you're writing from one of your character's perspectives? What could a character's diary reveal that a character sketch doesn't? Why is it useful to create material that won't be used in a narrative?

Part II: Plot

15

Originality

Originality isn't about coming up with something that's never been done before, although if you can pull that off, more power to you. Originality is about mixing and matching plots, characters, settings, and themes in a way that feels fresh.

If you look closely at most stories, you'll find that many elements within them have appeared in stories that came before. Stories are made from a bunch of different ingredients. You can remove a few ingredients and add a few ingredients, and you'll have a new recipe in hand. But you're still using the same basic ingredients that have been around forever.

The secret to good storytelling isn't to come up with a new ingredient—but if you get the balance of ingredients right by mixing them together in a new way, your story will be pretty tasty.

Consider a story about an orphan being raised by his aunt and uncle: He is called on a fantastic adventure where he meets strange and wondrous creatures and learns that he possesses special powers. He is tasked with defeating an evil lord with whom he has a dark connection. That's a simple summary of Harry Potter's tale, but it's also the story of Star Wars, and if you keep looking, you'll find many more similarities between these two stories (like the hero's sidekicks falling in love with each other!). Yet a casual reading and viewing of these stories doesn't immediately connect them. That's because the ingredients were mixed up just right to make something fresh.

Study:

Continue the comparison of Harry Potter and Star Wars. What other similarities can you find between these two iconic stories? What are the significant differences that make the stories so distinct that it's not obvious that they share so many likenesses? As an alternative, find two other stories that share a lot of similarities but seem original, and list their similarities and differences. As you continue with your studies in storytelling, always be on the lookout for plot structures, characterizations, settings, and themes that you've seen elsewhere.

Practice:

Create a simple outline for a story with about twelve plot points. Include a protagonist, an antagonist, and at least three additional primary characters. Keep the details vague.

Write a five-hundred-word summary of this story with lots of detail.

Then write another five-hundred-word summary of this story, but make it totally different from the first summary you wrote.

Your goal is to use the same basic story structure or premise to develop two stories with hidden, but significant, similarities.

Questions:

Can you think of any other stories with significant similarities? Do they share a similar structure or similar components? Do you think authors ever accidentally write stories with striking similarities to other stories? How often do you think writers develop stories only to later learn that something they thought was original has already appeared in some other story that came before?

16

Plot Types

In his book *The Seven Basic Plots*, Christopher Booker identified seven plots, summarized as follows:

- **Overcoming the Monster:** The protagonist tries to overcome an antagonist (which can be a character or a force).

- **Rags to Riches:** The protagonist acquires something they didn't have before (love, money, etc.).

- **The Quest:** The protagonist goes on a journey to acquire something important.

- **Voyage and Return:** The protagonist visits a strange land, overcomes various challenges there, and returns home.

- **Comedy:** Humorous story with a happy ending in which the protagonist triumphs.

- **Tragedy:** The protagonist's flaws or mistakes lead to a negative outcome.

- **Rebirth:** Events cause the protagonist to undergo significant and meaningful personal transformation.

If you analyze almost any story, you'll find that it fits into one of these seven plot types. Some stories might fit into two or more. For example, a quest can also be a comedy.

These plot types aren't literal: in "Overcoming the Monster," the hero is attempting to defeat an antagonist, but the antagonist isn't necessarily a monster in the literal sense: An asteroid hurtling toward Earth could be the monster. "Rags to Riches" is more about a protagonist obtaining something they desperately want; it doesn't have to be material wealth (many romances are rags-to-riches stories).

Study:

Make a list of about a dozen of your favorite stories, and then assign the plot types listed above to each to one. If a story contains more than one plot type, list them all. When you're done, highlight any plot types you didn't assign to a story, and then try to think of a story that fits it. If you're feeling adventurous, identify the subplots in the stories you've listed, and assign plot types to those as well.

Practice:

Develop one-paragraph story summaries for at least three (but preferably all) of the seven plot types. If you're feeling inspired, write one-page synopses, outlines, or full stories.

Questions:

Can you think of any stories that don't fit into any of these plot types? Are you aware of any other systems for categorizing plot types? What is it about these seven plot types that appeals to the human psyche?

17

Concepts and Premises

The premise of a story can be summed up in a few words: *imagine a world in which robots have taken more than half of all jobs.* A premise sets the stage and gives us a vague idea of what a story is about, but it doesn't tell us the specifics. Concepts get into specifics.

There are two kinds of concepts: high and low. A low concept is stripped down and generic: *a man loses his job to a robot.* A high concept adds interest and details that inspire interest in a story: *When half of the population finds itself jobless as a result of automation, one man raises a rebellion to seize resources essential to survival.*

Note the key differences between premises and concepts: Premises paint a vague picture of a story world and situation. Concepts identify key points, such a protagonist, an antagonist, a setting, and a central story question or problem (plot).

Premises and concepts have two important uses: developing and selling a story. Storytellers often start with a premise or concept as the first seed of a story idea. Later, concepts and premises can be worked into juicy statements about a story that can be used for pitching to agents, editors, and readers.

Study:

Make a list of ten stories. For each story, write a one-sentence premise and a one-sentence concept. Your concept statement can be high or low (some stories will only fit one or the other). Some stories contain multiple premises and concepts; for this exercise, identify the central concept and premise. Set the exercise aside for a day or two, and then reread the definitions above of concepts and premises and double-check your work.

Practice:

Set a timer for ten minutes, and create as many premises as you can in that time. If you're struggling to come up with ideas, use starters such as "what if..." or "imagine a world in which..."

Next choose two of your premises; develop one into a low concept, and develop the other into a high concept. Communicate your concepts in no more than two sentences (preferably one sentence).

Questions:

Have you ever started a story with a premise? What about a concept? If you start with characters, situations, themes, or some other seedling, when does concept or premise become part of your story development? Do you think concept and premise are important for communicating the essence of a story?

18

Inciting Incidents and Narrative Hooks

Most stories start with introductions: You meet the main characters and get a sense of the story's setting and background. At some point, early in the story, the inciting incident occurs. This is the event that kicks off the story's core conflict, challenge, or problem. It lets readers know what the primary plot is about.

The inciting incident changes everything for the protagonist, obstructing their progress or pushing them onto a new path. It is the first major change, or turning point, in the story.

An inciting incident can double as a narrative hook, but a narrative hook doesn't have to be the inciting incident. A narrative hook is any event, action, or detail at the beginning of a story that hooks readers' attention to keep them turning the pages.

Both the inciting incident and a narrative hook occur near the beginning of a story, but the inciting incident establishes the core conflict whereas a narrative hook is designed to keep the audience interested in the story. They can occur at the same time in a story and can also be contained within a single plot point.

Study:

Make a list of ten short stories or novels that you've read. Look through the first few chapters or paragraphs, and find the inciting incident in each story. Write a couple of sentences explaining how this inciting incident establishes the central conflict and marks the first turning point (change) in the story. Try to find narrative hooks in the stories you've listed, and note those as well.

Practice:

Using the starter phrase "This story is about…" write a list of five to ten story concepts, noting the inciting incident for each one. Add a short description of a narrative hook for at least half of the story ideas you've created.

Questions:

Why is the inciting incident important? Is the inciting incident always obvious? Must it always occur at the beginning of a story? Could a narrative hook be mistaken for an inciting incident?

19

Rising Tension

In music there's a concept called crescendo. Technically it refers to a gradual increase in loudness or intensity. But there's an emotional component too. As a piece of music approaches crescendo, the emotional quality intensifies—the music and lyrics grow sadder, angrier, or more celebratory. In most songs, there are multiple crescendos. There's buildup, then things slow down, then more buildup, then things slow down again.

Stories follow a similar pattern in what we refer to as rising tension. Stories move toward a central climax, which is when the story reaches the moment of maximum tension—this is where the stakes are at their highest, the emotions are at peak intensity, and the central story problem is about to be resolved.

But if you look closely, you'll see that there are smaller crescendos throughout most stories. Even as the tension rises and falls, there is an underlying current of tension that builds up, up, and up until we get to the climax.

Study:

Conduct an analysis of rising tension in a story by making a list of moments of peak tension—these are moments with a buildup in tension before a peak occurs and a decrease of tension follows. Then make a list of moments in which tension relating only to the central conflict (the main plot) increases. If you're feeling creative, make a rough sketch of a line chart, which will help you visualize the patterns of tension in a story.

Practice:

Come up with a simple story concept, and then create a series of plot points in which the tension increasingly rises to a moment of climax. For example, a woman goes for a hike in the woods with her dog. The dog runs off (tension rises). She sets off in pursuit and eventually realizes she's thirsty and out of water (tension rises again). Then she realizes she's lost (tension rises even more). She has no cell phone signal (tension continues to rise). It gets dark (tension rises yet again). She hears an animal growling nearby (moment of maximum tension).

Then try this exercise with a more complex structure by

building in rising and falling tension. For example, if the woman finds a stream, it will relieve some of the tension that built up when she realized she was out of water. Don't resolve every moment of tension, otherwise there won't be a steady increase of tension as the story moves toward the final climax.

Questions:

Why is rising tension so common in storytelling? Do you think it's necessary to any good story? Which do you think is preferable, consistently rising tension or tension that ebbs and flows as it rises to maximum tension? Can you think of any stories without rising tension? If not, what would a story without rising tension look like?

20

Subplots

Subplots enrich a story, allowing the narrative to delve deeper into the central plot, the story world, or the characters and their relationships. Good, strong subplots explore nuances of a story and the world it inhabits. The most effective subplots are intertwined and closely related to the core plot and theme, enriching the story by providing deeper information about it.

Lord of the Rings is primarily about the One Ring and the mission to destroy it in the fires of Mount Doom to save all of civilization. The story is full of subplots—most notably the friendship between Frodo and Sam, which develops and strengthens throughout the story. This subplot is intricately tied to the central plot because Sam is accompanying Frodo on his journey to bring the ring to Mount Doom, and he contributes to the mission in essential ways. The emotional nature of the subplot combined with its pertinence to the central plot makes it robust and appealing.

Weak subplots are usually random tangents, often the result of the author following an idea that isn't essential to the story, or they are offshoots of the central plot that offer no value, benefit, or interest to the story or the reader.

Study:

Identify the core plot in five (or more) of your favorite stories. Identify as many subplots as you can in each one. Then choose one of the stories, and for each subplot, write a sentence or two explaining whether the subplot was necessary to the story and how it made the story stronger or weaker.

Practice:

Develop a series of subplots around a very simple and straightforward central plot premise. For example, you could use a romance (a character is looking for love); a mystery (a detective is solving a crime); or a quest (a group of characters goes on a journey to obtain something important). Create three to five subplots for the plot premise you've chosen.

Questions:

Are subplots essential to a story? How can they be used to enhance a narrative? How many subplots are too many? How many are not enough?

21

Plot Points

Plot points are the events that move a story forward—the twists, turns, and developments that push the characters toward the climax and resolution. Each plot point is a significant moment in the grander scheme of things. If a character loses her keys as a way to show us she's absent-minded, then it's not a plot point (it's characterization). But if she loses her keys when she needs to drive to the emergency room in a life-or-death situation, then it becomes a plot point.

When we isolate the plot points in a story, we can see the plot without the distractions of characters, setting, or theme. Examining plot points in this manner allows us to look at the raw structure of the plot and can reveal its weaknesses: unnecessary repetition, plot holes, poor pacing, inconsistencies, lack of rising tension, and other problems that might require troubleshooting.

Breaking out the plot points is one way to examine a story in a condensed format, and you can use a map of a story's plot points to fix story problems before, during, or after writing a draft, which is more efficient than revising an entire manuscript.

Study:

Make a list of all plot points from a story you know well. Depending on your source material, you might want to work on just a chapter or two. You can also use a movie or an episode of a television show for this exercise. Review the story and double-check your list of plot points to make sure you've captured them all, and then perform an assessment. Make notes about what works in the plot and what could be improved.

Practice:

Create a series of plot points for a story. You don't have to plot the entire story—a simple subplot or enough material for a few scenes or chapters will do. Try to include an arc with a beginning, middle, and end. Keep other details as vague as possible. For example, don't spend time naming characters or establishing the setting. You can use generic terms like *protagonist* or *protag's BFF.* When you've got at least twelve plot points, set it aside for one day.

Come back to your plot points and review them. You'll probably find some problems—maybe one of the plot points is convoluted or contrived; maybe it feels like the story skips over a few plot points. Revise accordingly.

Questions:

Here are some questions to ask as you evaluate a plot: Would removing any of the plot points change a story's outcome? Are some plot points part of an important subplot, or are they all tied to the main plot? Do any plot points seem repetitive? Are any plot points unbelievable? Do any seem contrived or forced? Is anything missing—does the story skip over any necessary plot points?

22

Plot Backstory

All events that occurred prior to the current story are considered backstory. Backstory is usually revealed through exposition, dialogue, or flashbacks, and it has significant bearing on the current events within a story, explaining how things got to where they are now. Backstory adds depth and realism and enriches a story world with details from its past.

Authors often create backstories for their plots and characters to gain a deeper understanding of them. Details from these backstories might be used during story development but never revealed in the final narrative, or an elaborate backstory might be included in a narrative as a minor but essential detail.

Plot backstory is different from character backstory. A character's backstory describes the highlights of a character's life up to the moment that the story starts. A plot backstory looks at broader events in the story world that occurred prior to the story's beginning.

Plot backstory is particularly useful in complex stories, such as stories set in the distant future, family sagas (backstory would describe the family dynamics over previous generations), and historical fiction—to name a few.

Study:

Choose a novel you've read, and scan through it to find at least three examples of plot backstory. For each backstory that you find, note what occurred in the backstory, how it was revealed, and what relevance it has to the primary story.

Practice:

Develop a story premise and summarize it in about 250 words. Then write a plot backstory of about five hundred words describing the events leading up to the story.

Questions:

What are the benefits and drawbacks of the different methods of revealing backstory (dialogue, exposition, and flashbacks)? Why is it best to only include plot backstory if it's important to the story's central plot? Have you ever read backstory that was unnecessary or irrelevant? Why would it be helpful to create backstory for a plot but then leave most details of the backstory out of the manuscript?

23

Loglines and Taglines

Loglines hail from the film industry. A logline is a short and concise summary of a movie that's designed to pitch it to a director, a producer, or in the case of television, a network. Loglines often appear as short descriptions to help audiences understand what a film or television show is about. They are usually a single sentence—two sentences at the most. They set expectations for the story by presenting key details: the protagonist, the antagonist, and the central story problem are revealed. Here are some examples from the Internet Movie Database (IMDB):

Titanic: A seventeen-year-old aristocrat falls in love with a kind but poor artist aboard the luxurious, ill-fated RMS *Titanic*.

The Dark Knight: When the menace known as the Joker wreaks havoc and chaos on the people of Gotham, the Dark Knight must come to terms with one of the greatest psychological tests of his ability to fight injustice.

Hidden Figures: The story of a team of African-American women mathematicians who served a vital role in NASA during the early years of the US space program.

The Big Bang Theory: A woman who moves into an apartment across the hall from two brilliant but socially awkward physicists shows them how little they know about life outside of the laboratory.

Don't confuse a logline for a tagline, which is a pitch that is specifically targeted to audiences. Taglines appear on posters and other publicity materials. They are designed to arouse curiosity and inspire interest in a film rather than reveal key details about it. Here are a few examples of taglines:

Alien: In space, no one can hear you scream.

Jurassic Park: An adventure 65 million years in the making.

Office Space: Work sucks.

Loglines are occasionally used in the publishing world too. They can come in handy when you need a short and pithy description for your book on social media or marketing materials. And taglines aren't just for movies—plenty of product manufacturers and service providers use them alongside branding. Authors can make good use of loglines and taglines too.

Study:

Make a list of five of your favorite films, and then find the loglines for each one (you can find loglines on the IMDB website). Try to find a mix of genres to get a taste of how loglines might be written for different target audiences. For each logline, answer the following questions: Does it accurately describe the story? Does it tell us something about the antagonist, protagonist, and central story problem? Does it inspire interest in the story?

Do a little further research to see if these five films also use taglines, and note those as well.

Practice:

Make a list of your five favorite novels and then write your own loglines for each one. Then write a tagline for each one. When you're done, review your work. Do the loglines reveal interesting details about the stories? Do the taglines inspire interest? If not, revise accordingly.

If you've written any novels or are currently working on any stories, write loglines for those as well.

Questions:

How is a logline different from a concept or premise, or is it? Could the text used for a concept or premise also be used for a logline? What makes a tagline effective?

24

What If?

"What if?" is a useful prompt at any stage in story development. We can use this question as a story starter for an initial idea, and then we can continue to use it for plot development, characterization, and more.

What if the bones of a fire-breathing, flying dinosaur were discovered buried inside a mountain? What if a political strategist was being blackmailed by someone within their own party? What if scientists discovered a habitable planet outside of our solar system? What if a lonely, older widower fell in love with his married neighbor? What if a sidekick in a story turned out to be working for the antagonist? What if you chose a random moment in your story—a point where a character makes a choice—and let the character choose a different path?

"What if?" is a powerful tool that you can use throughout the story writing process, especially when you're stuck. You can write lists of what-if questions and answer them with quick sentences to get ideas for where you could steer a story.

Study:

Make a list of ten stories that you've read. For each one, come up with a "what if?" question that could have inspired the entire tale. Then choose one of the stories from your list, and come up with ten "what if?" questions that could have led to various character traits, actions, events, and situations that occur throughout the story.

Practice:

Make a list of ten what-if scenarios that could form the basis for a story. Then choose one, and build on it with at least eight more what-if questions.

Questions:

What if the central plot of your story works better as a subplot? What if a character isn't who they appear to be? What if you flip the ending of your story to the opposite outcome? What if your characters make different choices or have different goals? What if the protagonist's goals align with the antagonist's goals—who or what becomes the new antagonist?

25

Page-Turners

Page-turners aren't for everyone. Some readers feel like a cliffhanger at the end of every scene or chapter feels like the author is trying to manipulate them, and that's not entirely off the mark. But other readers love a good page-turner, the kind of book that keeps them up all night—the kind of book they can't put down because every time they get to the end of a chapter, they just have to find out what happens next.

So how do you create that kind of story?

The word *cliffhanger* comes from scenes, chapters, or books that end at a critical moment, such as a character hanging from the edge of a cliff, leaving the audience on the edges of their seats. Will the character fall to her death? Will someone save her? Will she save herself? What happens next?

But there are other ways to keep readers turning pages. For example, you can introduce new and intriguing story questions at the end of a scene or chapter. This is especially useful if the story has recently answered an open question or solved a problem or mystery. You don't have to leave your character on death's doorstep: an ongoing cascade of questions, problems, and mysteries will hold readers' attention.

Let's say you're writing a romance novel about a protagonist and his love interest. They can't be together because they work for competing companies, and the protagonist's love interest is married. There are a number of ways you could create moments that will keep readers turning the pages: the love interest's spouse confesses to having an affair or asks to renew their vows; the protagonist meets a second love interest, creating a love triangle; someone discovers their romance and threatens to destroy their careers.

Surprises also hold readers' attention, especially when things or characters aren't what they appear to be. For example, let's say the protagonist in this romance story discovers that his love interest isn't married after all; she's been lying to him this whole time.

Moments that keep readers turning pages are often turning points in a story that cause the tension to rise, which has the added benefit of creating emotional interest and intensity.

Cliffhangers and page-turning moments don't work for every story, and if not executed well, they can make a narrative feel contrived. So they should only be used if they flow naturally within a story.

Study:

Think about some stories you've read in recent years. Did any of them include cliffhangers? Browse through some of your favorite stories, and find at least five examples of cliffhangers. Choose two from your list, and then write a brief essay of about five hundred words comparing, contrasting, and analyzing them. Were they effective? Why? Were they necessary to the story, or did they feel like cheap tricks to keep readers glued to the page?

Practice:

Create a simple story concept, and then develop two cliffhangers and three other page-turning moments that could be worked into it.

Questions:

Which of the readers' emotions or sensibilities do cliffhangers appeal to? Do you prefer page-turners over other types of stories? Why do some people dislike cliffhangers while others love them? What kind of stories wouldn't work as page-turners? Do any genres lend themselves especially well to cliffhangers and page-turning moments?

26

Plot Twists and Reversals

Who doesn't love a good plot twist? A surprising or unexpected change in a story's direction grabs a reader's attention. It's a wake-up call: things are about to get interesting.

Plot twists can come across as contrived or forced if they're unbelievable or too convenient. There's a fine difference between taking a story in an unexpected but compelling direction and pushing it off course.

Consider a murder mystery: The victim's bloody dress is found in the back of her closet, gashed with a hunting knife. Her personal belongings—purse, keys, wallet, and cell phone—are in her apartment. A teapot filled with water is screaming on the stove. But the woman is gone. The detectives find clues, and a few suspects emerge. The investigation lasts weeks. Then a discovery is made: The bloody dress didn't belong to the alleged victim after all, and the blood on it isn't hers either. This plot twist takes the story in an exciting new direction.

A reversal occurs when the characters or the direction of events in a story undergo a dramatic and polar change, often unexpectedly. Reversals are similar to plot twists, and a reversal may in fact be a plot twist. They bring an element of surprise.

For example, if a character has spent the entire story on a quest for hidden treasure and suddenly decides to give up the quest to save the commoners from a dragon, the character has undergone a reversal.

Study:

Make a list of five plot twists from some of your favorite stories. Include at least one reversal that primarily affected a character rather than the plot. Write a brief summary of each twist or reversal, describing where the story appeared to be going and how the plot twist or reversal changed its direction.

Practice:

Sketch out a story scenario, and zero in on a scene in which a plot twist or reversal could occur to bring dramatic flair and an element of surprise to the narrative. Then write the scene, making it two to five pages.

Questions:

Why are plot twists and reversals so compelling? Have you ever encountered a plot twist or a reversal that was a dud? Plot twists and reversals don't occur in all stories, but are they common in some genres or rare in others?

Part III: Setting

27

Setting It Up

Readers need to know when and where a story takes place. A story's setting is often established with description, which is essential in genres like historical, fantasy, and science fiction; these stories are set in worlds other than the familiar world we all know, so description helps readers better visualize the story world.

But describing a setting in a way that keeps readers interested isn't easy. Lengthy paragraphs about rural landscapes or interior decor quickly grow dull, especially if these settings are familiar to the readers.

Too much information can overwhelm readers, and skimping on details can leave them confused. The right amount of detail provides just enough information that the readers can visualize the setting while leaving room for their imaginations to fill in the rest. And that's a good thing—engaging readers' imaginations is what sets reading apart from other forms of storytelling, but it's important to give readers a foundation, something to build on. For example, if your story is set on a spaceship, readers probably don't need to know the color of the dials on the navigation system. However, they do need an overall sense of the ship—is it sleek and sterile, or is it dingy and banged up?

Description isn't the only way to establish setting. Details about any setting can be woven into a story's action and dialogue, with the characters discussing their surroundings and interacting with their environment.

Establishing the setting early in a story ensures that readers can visualize the story with greater ease, and using active language makes a setting more memorable.

Use action: Instead of describing busy streets packed with shoppers, show readers that *shoppers coursed through the city streets like rats in a maze*.

Show characters interacting with the environment: *Kate craned her neck and saw a tiny patch of sky amid the towering skyscrapers.* This simple action reveals that the scene is set in a big city.

In establishing time, you can simply state the date (*the year was 2012*), or you can place something in the setting that identifies the era: *A brand-new 2012 Porsche sped by, and Kate whirled on her heels just in time to see it disappear around the corner of Lexington.*

Study:

Find a passage in a story that establishes the setting, and then make a list of details that it includes. For example, a passage of description might mention a red chair, a golden candelabra, and a mahogany grand piano. Close your eyes and visualize the setting for a few moments. Then write a second list of details that your imagination provided.

Practice:

Write one to three paragraphs of description to establish a story's setting. Aim for language that is compelling, and describe the setting in a way that is interesting and engaging.

Then write a short scene that reveals further details about the setting. Use action and dialogue to reveal the setting.

Choose the details carefully. Your goal is to bring readers into the story world—let them see it, but make sure there's room for them to use their imaginations. Don't forget to include details that tell readers when the story takes place.

Questions:

Why is it important for readers to be able to visualize a setting early in a story? Could some settings be established in a sentence or even a few words? What kind of settings require more elaborate descriptions? How do you, as an author, decide which details to provide and which ones to let readers fill in with their imaginations?

28

Set in Time

An aspect of setting that is often overlooked is time—*when* a story takes place. This is an element of setting that historical authors pay close attention to, often conducting deep research to get every detail right—the clothes, the methods of transportation, and the society and culture as it existed at a particular moment in history.

But even authors of contemporary fiction must remain cognizant of a story's timeline. When do the story events occur? What year? What season? What time of day?

In addition to establishing when a story takes place, we

need to make sure readers always know where they are in a story's timeline. If there's a scene jump, did an hour pass? A day? A month? How do readers know?

Amateur authors often mark time by repeatedly stating when each scene takes place. It's Monday or Wednesday, ten a.m. or six p.m. These repeated mentions of time can make readers feel like they should be keeping track of the timeline on a calendar. Establishing the time is best done subtly, unless the story requires concrete statements of time, as might be the case in a detective story or spy thriller.

Keeping readers in a story's timeline without constantly reminding them of the day, month, year, or hour can be tricky. In most cases, all that matters is when the scene occurs in relation to a story's timeline. So once the base timeline is established (hopefully at the beginning of the story), we can use various cues to help the reader understand how time is passing. Common techniques include phrases such as "a month later," "the next day," and "later that evening." However, descriptions of the setting can also provide cues to inform readers about the time: the sun is rising, the moon is in the sky, the harvest has begun.

Study:

Find a story that spans a lengthy timeline, such as a generational saga. Make a list of ten significant time jumps in the story, with the first item on your list being when the story starts. For each time jump, find the sentence, paragraph, or phrase that establishes when the scene is set. Jot down a few words about the technique the author used to keep readers informed about the story's location in its own timeline.

Practice:

Spend a few minutes developing a rough timeline for a story of your own. Make sure it spans at least three years and jumps to at least seven different points in time. Each time marker will denote when a scene takes place. Example: June 1977, evening; August 1977, afternoon; January 1978, morning. For each of these time markers, write a few sentences that establish a scene within the timeline.

Questions:

Have you ever become confused about a story's timeline? This might be expected if you're reading a time travel story, but what about other types of stories? Have you ever been reading a story and grown tired of the narrative constantly telling you what day, month, year, or hour it was in each scene?

29

Opportunities and Limitations

A story's setting can present the characters with opportunities or limitations. Imagine a character gouging a knee while deep in the woods and without medical supplies versus such an injury in a city, where there's a hospital nearby. Imagine two characters who dream of becoming Broadway stars, but one lives in New York and the other lives in Arizona. If a character needs to bury something, but she lives on the tenth floor of a high-rise in a big city, she's got a logistical challenge that wouldn't exist if she lived on a farm in the Midwest.

You might choose a particular setting for your story because of the opportunities or limitations it provides. Many horror stories are set in the woods, which are easy to depict as scary and creepy, especially at night. Or you might choose a setting and later benefit from the opportunities or limitations it presents your characters; or perhaps the setting you've chosen will impede the narrative that you've planned, and you may need to move the story to a different location.

This is why it's important to think about how your story's setting will affect your characters' daily lives and the challenges they will face.

Study:

Think about all the stories you've read, and list five scenes in which a story's setting imposed limitations on the characters. Then list five scenes in which a story's setting provided opportunities for the characters.

Practice:

Here are five story settings: a space shuttle; a submarine at sea; an abandoned ghost town; aboard a ten-hour transcontinental flight; a tiny village in the jungle. For each of these settings, make a list of five opportunities and five limitations. Then choose one of these settings, and write a scene set in that location, showing the characters facing one limitation and seizing one opportunity that their environment presents.

Questions:

How is a character affected by their location or the time in which they live? Can you think of any stories in which the setting is mostly irrelevant? What kinds of challenges or opportunities might a setting offer you, as a storyteller? Have you ever written a story and had to make adjustments to the setting because it was interfering with your narrative in an undesirable way?

30

Props

Often when we talk about setting, we forget an important element: props. These are the items that appear in the narrative and are part of the story world.

In real life, props are crucial. Think about how your day starts: Your alarm clock goes off, you use the toilet, start the coffeemaker, hop in the shower, then scarf down breakfast so you don't miss the bus to work. But what if your story is set in the eighteenth century? They didn't have alarm clocks, toilets, or coffeemakers. If you're writing historical fiction, you need to know the details of everyday objects and how people used them, and you need to think about which ones are important to include in your story. You may never need to show how characters bathed in the eighteenth century; on the other hand, you might want to include a steamy bath scene in your narrative.

If you're writing fantasy or science fiction, you may need

to invent your own props, and you might find yourself naming things that didn't exist until you thought them up.

In contemporary fiction, we don't need to give much thought to props. The story takes place in the real world that we all know, so we would expect to see computers, mobile phones, cars, and a host of other items that we are accustomed to using. But as authors, we still need to think about which props are necessary to a story, which props will enrich a story, and which can go unmentioned.

Study:

Revisit a story you've recently read. Without looking at it, try to list at least ten props that appeared in the story. For each one, write a few words about the significance of that prop to the narrative. Was it just part of the setting? Was it used in the action? Was it essential to the story? Did it enrich the narrative in some way? Now flip through the story, and find ten more items and answer the same questions about those.

Practice:

Quickly sketch a story summary. Keep it to about 250 words or fewer. Include the time and place, the story's general concept and premise, at least three key characters, and a few sentences describing the plot. Don't try to come up with a masterpiece—just keep it simple. Now make a list of fifteen items that would appear in the story. Five of these items will be part of the story's setting but not essential to the plot. Another five items will be objects that the characters use or interact with. The final five items will be absolutely necessary to the story.

Questions:

How do props provide important clues about a story? Should all props be necessary to a story in some way? What can props tell us about the setting, plot, and characters? How can props be used in place of description or exposition?

31

Model Locations

Whether you're writing an epic fantasy in space or a contemporary romance set in a suburban town, it's important to visualize your story's location. Where is the market in relation to the protagonist's house? Is there a river nearby? Where do people in town work? What kind of resources are available to them? Your story could be set inside a single house or it could sweep across a vast galaxy—as an author, you need to know where everything's happening.

Using a model for your location is just one of several methods you can employ to develop a story's setting.

Let's consider an epic fantasy that's set in a world with a medieval European flair. Since nobody's invented a functional time machine yet, you can't actually visit the time and location your story world is based on. That's where research comes in handy. You can interview experts in medieval European history, read history textbooks and historical novels, and watch films and documentaries about medieval Europe. And if you can get to Europe to scout locations, all the better. Although you won't be in the same era as your story, you can still survey various locations to get a firsthand sense of how things are laid out.

What if you're writing contemporary fiction? You can set your story in a real city or a made-up one. But even if you use a made-up city, you can use a model for your location—whether it's New York City or a one-road town deep in the country. Ideally, you'll be able to visit any real location that you're using as a model for a story's setting, but if travel's not in your budget, you can use maps and videos to study the location, and you can connect with people who live there to get insider tips from locals.

If you're inventing a place, you can use any city or town as a model, including places that are near wherever you live.

Study:

Choose a book, movie, or television show that's not set in a real location, and write a five-hundred-word essay explaining how you think the creators might have used real-world models for the story's setting. This isn't a test, so you don't have to get it right. The goal is to use your imagination to figure out how a creator might have researched and developed a location using real places as models.

Practice:

Sketch some ideas for a setting that you'll design for a story. Don't worry about characters or plot. This is about time and place. It should be a location you've never visited. Some ideas to get you started: a penthouse apartment in New York City, a farm in the rural Irish countryside, a film studio in Hollywood, a village on a tropical island, a carnival caravan in the nineteenth century, a spaceship traversing the galaxy in the distant future.

Find a location to use as your model, and then conduct research on the setting you've chosen.

Take some time to think about how you'll customize the location you've researched for your story. Maybe you found a model apartment that has a sleek, minimalist decor but you're going to give a traditional style makeover.

Finally, write a thousand-word description of the setting.

Questions:

Going beyond your personal experience, how many locations do you think you've visited in books? Movies? Television shows? Have you ever made up a place using your imagination? If you need to set a story in a location that is nothing like any place you've visited, what steps can you take to render a setting that is realistic and believable? How can you capture the essence of a place without having been there? What are the benefits of using places as models but bringing in your own details to customize them for your story? Do you prefer to use real locations or made-up settings?

32

Setting as Character

Settings that have a personality of their own are popular with readers. Many science-fiction and fantasy stories are set in places that function as characters within the story: Harry

Potter's Hogwarts, the USS *Enterprise* from *Star Trek*, and Pandora from *Avatar* are a few good examples. But cities, towns, and rural landscapes can also have personalities. For example, New York has been called the fifth main character in the television series *Sex and the City*. Houses, vehicles, cities, planets, nations, and rooms can express distinct personalities.

Settings that behave like characters aren't appropriate for every story, but such settings can enrich a story.

To give a setting personality, think about what makes characters seem human, even if they're not. Humans walk, talk, think, and feel. We express ourselves. We form relationships with others. We exhibit moods, attitudes, ideas, and beliefs. Ascribing traits that are normally reserved only for people or characters to a setting will make the setting more lifelike and give it greater prominence in the story.

Study:

Think of a setting from a book, movie, or television show that functioned as a character in the story. First make a list of five personality traits that are distinctly human that the setting exhibited. Then make a list of five scenes in the story in which the setting exhibited these personality traits.

Practice:

For this exercise, write a character sketch for a place. Make a list of its traits, including details about its personality, style, attitude, economics, and philosophy. Is it relaxed and laid-back or dark and dangerous? Is it elite or working-class? Does it hinder people or lift them up? Is it friendly to newcomers, or is it exclusive and distrustful of outsiders?

Then write a story summary, an outline, or a scene to show

off this setting's personality. Make sure you keep the focus of the story on the plot and characters.

Questions:

Under what circumstances would a story call for a setting that functions as a character? Can you think of any other books, movies, or television shows in which the setting had its own personality?

33

World-Building

For some authors, world-building is the most exciting step in the process of writing a story. Think about it—you get to create an entire world from scratch. You choose the landscape, the social structure, the government, and the culture. You can design maps, and you'll probably develop a world history. You are the master of this world, which is pretty powerful, even if it exists only in your head (and in your manuscript).

Some authors skip this entire process, of course. They write their stories, and the world takes shape alongside the narrative. In many cases, world-building is unnecessary because the story is set in the contemporary world. But many authors, particularly in the fields of science fiction and fantasy, spend a lot of time developing a rich and vibrant world in which their stories will be set. Historical authors may do something similar, but their world-building is based on research whereas science-fiction and fantasy authors can mix their imaginations with research on history and futurism.

There are plenty of things to consider when building a world, starting with the location and time. Does the story take place on a distant planet in another galaxy, in a fantasy world, or on an alternative version of Earth? Is it set in the near future or a long time ago? What are the people like? Are they homogeneous or diverse? Are there multiple species? What languages do they speak? What religions do they practice? What are the major cities, and what are the rural areas like? What are the social advantages or disadvantages? Is there magic? What kind of technology exists? What is the government like? What about food, art, and music?

Study:

Choose a story set in a fantasy or science-fiction setting, and write a one-page description of the world, touching on the following details: time, location, demographics, technology or magic, government, and culture.

Practice:

Use the world-building worksheet provided in the appendix to develop a sketch of your own science-fiction or fantasy world. Be sure to complete the entire worksheet for this exercise.

Questions:

What are some of your favorite stories that are set in worlds radically different from the real one in which we all live? Do you prefer science fiction or fantasy, or do you like both equally or not at all? What makes some speculative worlds rich and vivid while others are lackluster or feel like settings that were cloned from other stories (or from our real world)? What key features are necessary for successful world-building? Finally, how does an author best weave these details through the narrative so the world comes alive in readers' minds?

34

Setting Transitions

One of most important functions of a story's setting is to make sure readers know when and where a story takes place. Setting may need to be established for each scene within a story, especially if it takes place across multiple locations or includes a lot of time jumps.

However, if the narrative is constantly repeating the time and location at the beginning of each scene, it can grow tedious and tiresome. It's helpful to practice writing a sentence or two of setting, which can then be woven, almost unnoticeably, into a story. Or try slipping the setting into the first couple of sentences of action and dialogue. Better yet, find cues you can use to tip off readers about where and when a scene takes place.

For example, *the hot sun was glaring in her eyes* reveals a lot of information about the setting: it's daytime, probably summer, and the character is most likely outdoors.

If a setting has already been established earlier in the story, a scene may only need a few words to remind readers where it takes place; for example, mentioning characters that are present in a scene will reveal the location if readers already know where those characters are within the story world.

Study:

Choose a novel you've recently read that features multiple settings, and flip through it, making a list of five scenes set in different times and places. Find the spot in each scene that reveals when and where it's taking place, and make notes about the cues that are provided. Then do a quick analysis of each cue: Was it too blatant (actually stating the time and place)? How far into the scene is the setting established? Can you think of a better way for the narrative to have indicated the setting?

Practice:

Make a list of five different settings that will be used in a single story. You can keep the list simple (Mary's house on a summer day, the park at the onset of autumn, the coffee shop on an early winter morning, etc.). Write five introductory paragraphs for scenes that will occur in these locations. Try to come up with interesting yet subtle indicators of the settings that will show readers when and where a scene is set without making it a distraction.

Questions:

Aside from blatantly stating the time and location at the beginning of every scene, what are some ways an author can reveal a scene's setting? Have you ever felt jarred by the way a narrative transitioned between locations? What stories have you read in which transitions between settings was so smooth, you didn't even notice them? Have you ever gotten confused about a story's setting, and do you think it was because you misread the cues or because the author didn't clearly communicate the setting?

Part IV: Theme

35

Motif

A motif is a recurring idea, element, or symbol in a story. A story can have multiple motifs, and they can be just about anything, including an oft-repeated word, phrase, or gesture.

Motifs serve a variety of purposes. Repeating elements of a story's setting can reinforce the tone, mood, or atmosphere. Repeating a character's behavior establishes their personality. Repetition of broad concepts can support—or even form—a story's theme.

The film *Titanic* is packed with motifs. Wealth is represented throughout the film with recurring images of expensive artwork, jewelry, and other finery. Oppression is another motif, which is represented with Rose being dominated by Cal, the third-class passengers trapped below deck as the ship sinks, and Jack barred from leaving the third-class accommodations to visit Rose in first class. This contrast in motifs (wealth and oppression) contributes to the film's thematic statement, which deals with the choice between freedom and security.

Motif can often be summed up in a single word: liberty, blood, love, water, power, money, and fear are just a few examples of motifs that could appear in a story.

Concrete images are often used to form an abstract motif. Let's say you want a motif of liberation in your story. You might include a bird flying free from a cage, a prisoner being released, and a hostage escaping captivity. While no single image is repeated, the concept or idea of liberation is echoed in each of these images.

Motifs don't have to be deep, serious, or even meaningful. Any repetition can form a motif, even the recurring appearance of a caterpillar in a children's story.

Study:

Choose a favorite book, movie, or television show. Make a list of all the motifs you can identify. Explain the meaning of each motif, and list the instances when it appeared in the story.

Practice:

Make a list of three motifs that could work together in a story. Choose one that is material (a rose), one that is intangible (dreams), and one that represents a big idea (freedom). Write a short summary of the story, explaining what it's about and how these motifs would be presented throughout the story.

Questions:

Do all stories contain motifs? Can you think of any that don't? Do you think motifs are important? Why or why not?

36

Theme

Theme is often described as the message of a story, but this description doesn't do it justice. Theme is also the central meaning of a story, its moral core, its subtext. It's what a story is about beyond the plot and characters. *To Kill a Mockingbird* is the story of a girl named Scout and her father, Atticus Finch, a white lawyer who defends an innocent black man in 1950s Alabama—that's the plot. But the story is about racial injustice—that's the theme.

The mockingbird is a symbol in *To Kill a Mockingbird*:

> "Mockingbirds don't do one thing except make music for us to enjoy. They don't eat up people's gardens, don't nest in corn cribs, they don't do one thing but sing their hearts out for us. That's why it's a sin to kill a mockingbird."

This dialogue uses a mockingbird to explain why it's wrong to convict, harm, or punish someone who's innocent; the allegory of the mockingbird speaks to the novel's theme. The story includes multiple innocent characters who are treated unfairly by their community—a motif that underscores and buttresses the theme of social and systemic injustice.

Theme goes beyond motif, exploring deeper meanings and asking questions about topics that are raised by motifs; when a story's theme and motifs are linked in meaningful ways, a story becomes richer and deeper.

When evaluating a story's theme, there is often no absolute or objectively correct analysis; a story's theme could be subjective, depending on how a reader interprets the narrative. Any of the following statements about the theme of *To Kill a Mockingbird* would be correct:

- It's about racial injustice in the American South during the 1950s.

- It's about bringing change to a community.

- It's about taking a moral stance that flies in the face of tradition, conventional thinking, and popular culture.

Taking a few moments to contemplate a story's motifs and themes is a good exercise to do with any book, movie, or television show. You don't always need to write down your findings, but doing so will help you clarify your thoughts and better understand the story and its inner workings.

Study:

Choose one book, one film, and one television show you're familiar with. Identify one central theme in each story. Write a detailed sentence describing the theme, starting with the words "It's about..." Then write a paragraph to support your argument as to why this is the correct theme.

Practice:

Make a list of three to five motifs, each expressed in a single word. Then develop a theme from your list of motifs, expressed as a sentence. Revise your motifs and themes until they are all nicely interconnected. Finally, write a few paragraphs describing a story that would encapsulate the motifs and theme you've chosen.

For example, motifs could be *money, career,* and *love*, and the theme could be *making personal sacrifice for love*. Your story might be about a parent who gives up a high-profile career and a big salary to spend more time with their children.

Questions:

When reading a book, watching a movie, or viewing a

television show, do you ever contemplate the motifs and themes that are presented? Has a theme ever jumped out at you as too obvious? Have you ever realized months or even years after reading a book that it contained motifs or themes that you didn't initially notice? When developing a story, how often do you think about theme? Do you think theme is present in all stories? Can you think of any stories with no theme?

37

Thematic Patterning

Thematic patterning is the distribution of theme and motif throughout a story. We've learned that motif is a recurring idea, element, or symbol in a story and that theme is the deeper meaning of a story. But how are motifs and themes executed in practice?

Thematic patterning is how we use repetition to drive home aspects of a story or the ideas it contains. It's not as simple as deciding that doves symbolize peace and then showing a dove flying overhead every time the story needs to emphasize peace as a motif. Assuming there's a good reason why doves are always flying around, this could work, but a motif can be made richer by subtle or nuanced repetition: A dove can appear in one scene, and an olive branch can appear in another. Both are universally recognized symbols of peace, and together they form a motif of peace.

Consider a story about two families living in America's Wild West who are engaged in a violent feud over a land dispute. If they manage to reach peace rather than massacring each other, the theme might be valuing human life over property. The thematic patterning would be formed with a combination of motifs, symbols, plot points, and characters. The repetition of motifs and the presence of symbols underscores ideas contained in the theme; plot points show the theme in action; and characters embody the theme through their behaviors and conversations.

Study:

Choose a story, and identify its theme. Write a one-page essay describing the story's thematic patterning. How did the story use motifs? What clues revealed the theme? How frequently were the theme and motifs represented?

Practice:

Start with a story premise or concept. You can use a story that you're already developing or create a new story idea. Then choose a theme for your story. Choose at least three motifs that will underscore the theme, five plot points that will establish the theme through action, and three characters who, through behavior and dialogue, will highlight or embody the theme. Finally, write a one-page essay describing how you will use thematic patterning to communicate the central idea of your story—its deeper meaning.

Questions:

What are some of the story elements that can be used to build thematic patterning? Why is patterning necessary to establish a story's theme? Is thematic patterning more effective when it's overt or subtle, or does it depend on the story?

38

Starting from Theme

More often than not, a theme manifests in a story without a writer putting much thought into it during early outlines and drafts.

Aspiring writers are often discouraged from focusing on theme and are instead encouraged to focus on building characters and plot—the theme will emerge naturally, and it can be fine-tuned during revisions. When a story's theme is at the forefront of a writer's mind, the story can become preachy, and the elements readers connect with (characters and plot) fall to the wayside, becoming mere instruments to deliver a message. This can result in a story that lectures readers and feels forced.

However, theme can be a useful tool in the writing and editing process. It certainly doesn't hurt to consider the underlying themes that might emerge from any story idea while it's in the development phase.

Starting from theme may not be an ideal way to develop a story, but it's a useful exercise for better understanding theme and its importance to any narrative.

Study:

Children's books often contain themes that are blatantly obvious, sometimes to the point of being preachy from the perspective of an adult reader. These can range from messages about sharing toys with friends and siblings to promoting healthy eating or hygiene habits. This isn't necessarily a bad thing. Stories with strong and obvious messages are appropriate for children as part of their development. Consider Dr. Seuss's *Green Eggs and Ham*, which is a fun, rhyming story that shows kids why it's important to try new things. The characters and plot aren't especially vivid or interesting, but the story is a blast to read; kids and adults alike love it.

Make a list of five to ten stories that evoke strong themes and clear messages to the point of being obvious in their messaging. Feel free to use children's books, but try to come up with at least one story for adult readers. For each story, note the message or theme. Then choose one of the stories you've listed, and write a short essay speculating how the author might have developed the story if the theme were its starting point. For example, did Dr. Seuss think to himself, *some kids are so finicky. I'm going to write a story encouraging them to try new things. What will the character in my story try? I know! Ham and eggs. Not just any eggs—green eggs.* This is meant to be pure speculation (although you're encouraged to conduct research after you complete the exercise and try to find out the genesis of the story you've used).

Practice:

Develop a list of three themes, and for each one, sketch ideas for how it could manifest through character, plot, or scenes.

Here's an example using a theme that examines revenge: A woman is fired because a coworker reported her for stealing. Instead of accepting responsibility for the consequences of her actions, she blames the coworker and gets him fired too. The coworker then lands an even better job at another company while the woman remains unemployed.

Go beyond a short synopsis—how could the theme be echoed in other elements of the story (setting, plot, characters)? What motifs could support the theme?

Questions:

Why do you suppose starting with theme often leads to stories that come across as preachy? Why do you suppose stories that aren't preassigned themes might produce richer and more interesting themes? Have you ever started with theme or motif, or do a story's motifs and themes usually emerge as you develop the narrative?

39

Theme Master

Understanding theme, learning to identify it in stories, and figuring out how to use it in your own work can lead to a more pleasurable experience as a reader and a deeper relationship with storytelling.

As you continue your work in writing fiction, you might find that when a story is completed and you reflect upon it, the theme is the most important element of all.

Study:

Now that you've learned how to identify themes and experiment with them in your own work, make a master list of themes that can be used in storytelling. Whenever you come across an interesting theme in a book or movie, add it to the list. Put an asterisk (or other marker) next to themes that you find most interesting and might want to explore in your own work.

Practice:

Find a story you've developed that's far enough along that a theme should have emerged. Perhaps you've written a detailed outline or completed a partial or full first draft. It could be a story that's not yet complete but is in its final stages. Write up an assessment of the motifs and theme. Are they connected or related in meaningful ways? Is there a consistent theme throughout the story, or does it meander through different themes? Could you make the motifs or theme stronger?

Questions:

Why do you think theme is considered one of the most important elements of fiction? What is the benefit of analyzing themes in stories? In the absence of readers spending considerable time or energy contemplating the themes of stories they've read, do you think they absorb the themes anyway? If a story contains a disagreeable theme or idea, are readers more likely to change their views or dislike the story (perhaps without even knowing why they dislike it)?

Part V: Structure

40

Chapters

First-time novelists often ask how many chapters should be in their books and how long the chapters should be.

There are no rules about how to break a story into chapters. Some authors write longer scenes, each comprising a single chapter. Others include several scenes in each chapter. Sometimes chapters are based on point of view, with each chapter moving to a different character's perspective. Chapters can be long or short, and a single novel could contain chapters of roughly equal lengths or of varying lengths. Some novels don't have any chapters.

So how does an author decide how to break a story into chapters?

Chapters breaks are usually placed at a point where there is a shift in the story. A moment of high tension that rouses the reader's interest and curiosity is often a good place to close a chapter because chapter breaks work well when they leave the reader wanting more.

A moment that transitions between characters and locations or through time can also be a good placement for a chapter break.

And in stories with a steady and even flow, chapters often end where there's a natural albeit subtle break or pause in the story's rhythm. Compare a novel to a song: A song might be broken into a verse, a chorus, a bridge, and an instrumental section, each with rising (or falling) tension. Find natural points in the story where the tension changes, and these could be good spots for chapter breaks.

Study:

Review a novel to study the chapter breaks. Note the following: What is the length (in pages) of each chapter? Do the chapters shift between characters' points of view? Do chapter breaks occur when the story moves to different locations? What is the tone and level of tension at the beginning and end of each chapter? Do chapters end when a story thread closes, or do chapters end at points when the reader's curiosity is piqued and they want more? Once you've answered these questions, write a short essay of about 250 words describing the author's methodology for dividing the story into chapters.

Practice:

Outline the first five chapters for a novel. The story will be written in third person and should include at least two points of view. At least one chapter should include more than one scene, and at least one chapter should end on a cliffhanger. Keep the outline simple, with one or two sentences summarizing each scene within the story. When you're done, review your work and write a few paragraphs about what you've learned about chapter breaks.

Questions:

When you're reading a novel, do you tend to put it down at chapter breaks, or do you put it down in the middle of a chapter? Do you notice chapter breaks? Do you read the chapter titles, or do they mostly go unnoticed? Have you ever been jarred out of a story by the placement of a chapter break? Have you ever encountered a story with chapter structuring that you found fresh, interesting, or unusual?

41

Scenes

A scene is a single stretch of narrative in which characters engage in an unbroken sequence of action and dialogue. Scenes are the most basic building blocks in storytelling. Each scene contains a story arc: a beginning, middle, and end. There should be some element of change within each scene. This change could be a minor but essential detail about a character or a revelation about a major plot point.

Here's a checklist of what usually happens in a scene: The setting is established; there's action and dialogue; a conflict occurs (major or minor); tension rises or falls; and there is a change of some kind (large or small). Each scene should also have essential relevance to the greater story.

Study:

Select three scenes from short stories or novels. You can use three scenes from a single story or scenes from different stories. Using the checklist above, analyze each scene, and then answer the following questions: Does the scene include all elements on the checklist? If not, would the scene be improved by including all of them? If the scene works without all elements, why did it work? Did you notice any other story elements that were included in each scene? How did the scene begin? How did it end? What changed?

Practice:

Write a scene that includes all elements from the scene checklist above. Aim for a thousand words.

Questions:

What distinguishes a scene from a chapter? What cues tell you that a scene is beginning or ending? What are some ways a story can transition from one scene to the next?

42

Sequences

A sequence is a series of scenes that are connected. A sequence can occur at a single setting within a story or across different settings. The scenes within a sequence can be presented consecutively, or the story can move away from a sequence and return to it later.

A common sequence found in stories is a car chase. Consider a police procedural: The cops are hunting for members of an organized crime ring. The car chase sequence might consist of three separate scenes, each from a different character's point of view and each containing its own arc. For example, the first scene shows cops sitting at a traffic light and then turning on the lights and sirens when the criminals' car passes; the scene ends as the cops pull into the street to chase the criminals. The next scene shows the criminals speeding through city streets, trying to get away from the police; this scene ends when they have finally shaken the cops. Then we see the police searching for the criminals and finally finding their car parked behind an old garage; the scene ends when the cops have finally trapped the suspects with barricades in the street.

In this same story, there could be another plot thread in which the lead detective is interviewing suspects and gathering evidence. The scenes in the car chase sequence could be interspersed with the detective's scenes, breaking up the sequence.

Either way, the sequence consists of multiple scenes, each with a beginning, middle, and end during which something changes.

Study:

Find a sequence within a story, and make a list of all the scenes it contains. The scenes can be consecutive or interspersed with other scenes. Make a note of what changes in each scene and what changes in the greater sequence of scenes.

Practice:

Outline a sequence of at least five scenes that are interrelated. Decide if your scenes will be consecutive or interspersed with scenes from another thread in the story (if so, include the alternating scenes in your outline, and increase your scene count to at least eight).

Questions:

Are sequences essential in a story? Could a story include simple scenes but no sequences? What kind of story threads will work better as single scenes versus sequences? Is it preferable to keep all scenes within a sequence in consecutive order, or is it better to break them up?

43

Framing

Framing devices are actions, scenes, and events that establish bookends for inner stories. Similarly, a frame story is a story that contains one or more stories within it.

The novella *The Turn of the Screw* is a frame story: the narrative starts with an unnamed narrator listening as a friend reads a manuscript written by a governess; the governess's manuscript is the central story.

Framing isn't commonly used in storytelling; most stories pull us into a single, primary narrative. But in some cases, two intertwined stories might use framing, or there might be a story within a larger story, and some stories might even contain multiple smaller stories within them.

Study:

Think of at least three novels or short stories that use framing devices. At least one should use action, scenes, or events to bookend an inner story, and at least one should be a frame story. If you can't think of any such stories, include film and television or conduct a search online for "stories that use framing devices."

For each of the examples that you find, answer the following questions: Is the framing device necessary to the story? How would the core story change if the framing device were removed? Could the contents within the framing device be relayed in a more effective way? Would the story be better without the framing device?

Practice:

Draft a rough summary or outline for a story that uses framing, but make sure the framing is essential to the story. In other words, the story works better with framing (as opposed to simply inserting framing unnecessarily).

Questions:

Why do you suppose framing devices, especially frame stories, are so rare? Do some genres better lend themselves to framing devices? Have you ever used a framing device in a story you developed? How many stories with framing devices have you read?

44

Narrative Arcs

An arc has a beginning, a middle, and an end. The events within an arc result in some kind of change for the story world, characters, or direction of the plot.

In serial or episodic storytelling, a story arc is an ongoing story line that spans multiple installments. An arc might last through several episodes of a television show or several issues of a comic book. In literature, an arc might stretch across multiple books in a series.

A narrative arc (or dramatic arc) is similar to a story arc, except it doesn't have to occur across multiple installments of episodic storytelling. A narrative arc is any arc within a story, including the central plot and any subplots. Narrative arcs can occur within a single scene or span across a sequence of scenes.

Characters also experience arcs when they undergo a progression of transformation.

That's a lot of different types of arcs. To make matters more confusing, the terms for story arcs, narrative arcs, and dramatic arcs are often used interchangeably.

Study:

You can use any type of story for this exercise: books, comics, TV shows, or films. Find a series that you've enjoyed, and examine a small sample of installments. For example, you can look at five episodes from a TV show or three novels from a series. Make sure you're using serials, which use ongoing stories across multiple installments, rather than episodic installments, which are separate but loosely connected.

Make a list of three to five story arcs found across the installments you examined. Do the arcs intertwine? Are they occurring simultaneously, or are they consecutive? How does each arc relate to the central plot?

Practice:

Create a set of three story arcs that would span multiple

novels in a series. If you're already working on a series, feel free to create arcs within your project.

For example, start by writing quick summaries of at least five novels in a series (about one paragraph each, highlighting the central plot of each installment). Then come up with the three arcs, each of which would span multiple novels.

As an alternative, you can develop ideas for a television or comic book series.

Questions:

What is the difference between a story arc and a dramatic arc? Why are story arcs effective in serial storytelling? How is a character arc different from a narrative arc? What types of arcs are most important in storytelling?

45

Three Acts

The three-act structure is one of the simplest and most effective ways to outline or analyze a story and its structure. The three acts are as follows:

1. Setup

2. Conflict

3. Resolution

In the first act, the plot and characters are established, and we learn what the central conflict is. It's roughly 25 percent of the story, but this is a guideline, not a rule.

The second act is the longest of the three acts, usually comprising about 50 percent of the narrative. In the second act, the story builds up to a climax in which the conflict hits a boiling point.

Finally, the third act resolves the conflict. The third act is usually about 25 percent of the story.

Study:

Choose five stories you've read, and break them into three-act structures by identifying the setup, conflict, and resolution for each one. Summarize each act in just a few sentences.

Practice:

Create five story premises, and quickly draft three-act outlines for each one. Use a single sentence to describe each of the three acts. A couple of examples are provided below.

Natural Disaster:

Act I: A natural disaster is impending.

Act II: The natural disaster claims the lives of half of Earth's population. The other half struggles to survive.

Act III: Earth's survivors rebuild.

Romance:

Act I: A teenager from a prestigious family falls in love with someone from the wrong side of the tracks.

Act II: The couple tries to hide their relationship, but eventually they are outed.

Act III: The teenager is forced to choose between love and access to the family's wealth and support.

Questions:

Why do you suppose the three-act structure is universally applicable to almost all forms of storytelling? Would it be possible to write a story with no setup, or with the setup at the end or in the middle? What happens if the three acts are rearranged? Can any of the acts be left out of a story?

46

Messy Middles

The second act, or middle of a story, is often the hardest to write. It's a lot easier to set up a story or resolve it than to take it through the murky middle, which is filled with ups and downs, rising tension, and a multitude of conflicts large and small. This is where many authors get disconnected and drift away from their projects (some never return), and because the middle is so hard to write, it can also be the weakest part of a story for readers.

Ideas might be plentiful when you're creating a setup or figuring out a resolution for your story. But carrying your characters through the complex twists and turns of the middle requires more time and mental effort. Or maybe you just need to work through more revisions or a more detailed outline for your story's middle.

The key is to stick with it.

Study:

Find a lengthy novel that you've read before (preferably

one you've read several times and are familiar with) that has a strong and engaging middle. Write a three-page analysis of it. The first page should be an outline that describes the turning points and story beats that form the story's middle. Write at least two pages analyzing why it worked well (or didn't).

Practice:

Create a three-act outline for a story. Write one-sentence summaries of the setup and resolution. However, write five to ten sentences that summarize events that will occur through the middle of the story.

Questions:

Why do you suppose many authors struggle with the messy middle of a story? Have you ever struggled with the second act of a story you've written? Have you ever abandoned a project somewhere in the middle? Of the three acts (setup, conflict, resolution), which do you find easiest? Hardest? What techniques can you use to push through the difficult second act if you find it challenging?

47

The Hero's Journey

In 1949 Joseph Campbell published *The Hero with a Thousand Faces*, which showed plot points and character archetypes that commonly occurred in myths, legends, and other tales across a multitude of cultures throughout history.

The Hero's Journey, which is sometimes called the Monomyth, had emerged—a formula for storytelling that had been discovered but not yet developed.

Campbell's original structure included seventeen stages; since then, the Hero's Journey has undergone many variations. For this exercise, we'll work with one of the most widely used versions, a twelve-stage story structure developed by Christopher Vogler. Here's a summary of Vogler's twelve stages of the Hero's Journey:

1. **Ordinary World:** We are introduced to the Hero in their home or starting place.

2. **Call to Adventure:** The Hero's world undergoes a dramatic shift, either by an external force (often the villain) or by some change within the Hero's heart or mind or situation.

3. **Refusal of the Call:** The Hero resists the Call to Adventure or refuses to accept a role in the forthcoming challenge.

4. **Meeting the Mentor:** The Hero meets someone with knowledge or experience and receives training or supplies that will be required for the adventure.

5. **Crossing the First Threshold:** The Hero finally accepts the Call and resolves to leave home to embark on the adventure, entering a new space or state of mind.

6. **Tests, Allies, Enemies:** The Hero acquires Allies (helpers). Foes are established, and allegiances are forged. The Hero is tested.

7. **Approaching the Underworld:** The Hero and their helpers get ready for the first big challenge.

8. **The Ordeal**: The Hero enters the underworld and faces death (this can be symbolic) but will emerge reborn or with a new understanding, ability, or purpose.

9. **Reward:** There is a Reward for overcoming the Ordeal and surviving the underworld.

10. **The Road Back:** The Hero prepares to return home; the last leg of the mission lies ahead. The tension is reaching its peak.

11. **The Resurrection:** There is a final obstacle or challenge at the climax. The stakes are higher than ever. The Hero makes a sacrifice, suffers a loss, or undergoes another death and rebirth.

12. **Resolution and Return:** The conflict is finally resolved. The Hero returns home (this can be a symbolic homecoming), having grown and bearing knowledge or items (treasure) that will change the world for the better.

The structure is not meant to be rigid. There can be some overlap, and some stages might be repeated or occur out of order. Elements within this story structure can be symbolic or metaphorical rather than literal; for example, a treasure could be newfound knowledge rather than material wealth.

The stages listed above are summarized; you can find the full twelve stages in Christopher Vogler's book *The Writer's Journey*.

Study:

Try to find at least three novels that were published in the past fifty years that follow the structure of the Hero's Journey. Choose one, and plug the plot points into the Hero's Journey outline above.

Practice:

Try using the Hero's Journey to create a story. You don't have to write a full manuscript; just outline twelve stages for a story adhering to the formula above. To fully employ the Hero's Journey, revisit the exercise "Archetypal Characters," and incorporate the archetypes into your outline.

Questions:

Why do you suppose the Hero's Journey is universally found in stories throughout history and in many cultures? Why does it appeal to audiences on a basic, human level? Can you think of any stories (or genres) that wouldn't (or shouldn't) use the Hero's Journey?

48

Story Beats

Beats is a screenwriting term, but it's useful for all storytellers and can be especially useful for novelists. This term sometimes has different meanings. Traditionally, beats are units of time that are used to measure the pacing of a screenplay in order to plan a film's run time.

The word *beats* is also used to refer to story units, each of which contains a single significant action.

Authors can use beats as a method of outlining a story before writing the first draft. Beat sheets can also be created during revisions to get an overview of a story and figure out its pacing, turning points, structure, and balance. Beats can be used to work through an entire novel, a single chapter, or a challenging scene.

Here's an example of a few beats for "Little Red Riding Hood":

- Little Red Riding Hood carries a basket of food through the woods to her grandmother's house.

- The Big Bad Wolf secretly follows Little Red Riding Hood.

- He approaches her and convinces her to tell him where she's going.

- He tells her to pick some flowers for her grandmother. She does.

- While she's picking flowers, the Big Bad Wolf goes to the grandmother's house.

The story itself includes a lot more detail, like action and dialogue and description. But as you can see, beats provide a broad overview of every point of action in a story.

Study:

Find a short story, and break it into beats. Summarize each significant action with a single sentence (two sentences at the most). Details should be sparse, so avoid adjectives and adverbs unless they are absolutely necessary. Stay focused on the story's essential points of action.

Practice:

Use beats to outline a chapter for a story you're developing (or create a new story concept for this exercise). Complete at least one page of beats.

Questions:

Have you ever outlined a story before writing it? Have you ever broken a story into beats or summarized a scene in order to troubleshoot it while you were revising? Can you think of any other ways beats could be used during story development or the writing process?

Part VI: Narrative

49

Character Action

Action and dialogue are the wheels that carry a story forward. We see the characters taking action; we observe their conversations; sometimes we get inside their heads where their innermost thoughts are revealed. Action and dialogue show the story unfolding before our eyes.

Some actions are significant at the plot level: The crime, the car chase, and the first kiss are all examples of actions within a story that are essential to moving the plot forward. But some actions are useful for helping readers understand the characters, which might move the plot forward in subtle but significant ways.

Action shows us what the characters are doing, whether they are unhappily pushing food around on a plate or excitedly chasing a culprit through city streets. Consider the following:

Kate was sad.

Kate cried.

Kate swallowed hard and brushed away her tears.

The first example tells us how Kate feels. The second example shows us how Kate feels. But the third example uses action so we can see for ourselves how Kate feels. Which of these sentences evokes the most vivid image of the story playing out in your mind?

Study:

Find a scene in a book, movie, or TV show in which the characters do not talk. Write an analysis of how the scene keeps you engaged without dialogue. Make notes about what the characters do and how their actions are important to the story. Does the scene reveal important details about the characters? Does it move the plot forward?

Practice:

Write an action scene in which there is no dialogue (including no thought dialogue). The scene should be about a thousand words. Before you begin, establish a scenario in which no dialogue would occur. Some possibilities include a scene in a library; two characters taken hostage who have been bound and gagged; or a prisoner in solitary confinement. Refrain from including the characters' thoughts or dialogue. Keep any necessary description to a minimum.

Questions:

How do characters' actions in a scene enrich a story? Is there a difference between minor actions, like a character who constantly bites their nails, and major action, like fist fights?

50
Action Scenes

The love scene. The car chase. The fight sequence. These are all types of action scenes that usually mark important milestones that move a story's plot forward.

Action scenes are difficult to write because they require clear, detailed descriptions of each action the characters take. The narrative can't say the characters fought, Jake won, and Mitch ended up in the hospital. It must show the fight—establishing what the fight is about; how it starts; each punch, kick, and tackle; and the outcome. Later, it will probably delve into the aftermath—the consequences of the fight.

Poorly crafted action scenes often lack clarity. Readers get lost among too many or too few details and are confused by unclear details.

Action scenes can also suffer from poor pacing, especially when they are out of step with the surrounding narrative. If it takes an hour to read about the character riding her motorcycle to the ransom drop-off point and the fight that ensues takes only five minutes to read, there could be a serious problem with pacing where important moments in the story are given less time and weight than less significant moments.

Description and relevant details are also critical in action scenes. The readers need to be able to visualize every punch and kick. If it's unclear who's punching or who's getting kicked, readers will have a hard time following along.

Paying close attention to clarity, pacing, and description within action scenes is essential and will mean the difference between a riveting action scene and an action scene that tanks.

Study:

Make a list of five action scenes from some of your favorite stories. Then pick one and analyze it. What are its strengths and weaknesses? Examine the clarity, pacing, and description.

Can you follow the entire scene without getting confused about who's doing what? How would you improve it?

Practice:

Write an action scene that's about 750 words. You can create a new story scenario for this exercise or write an action scene for a story you're working on.

Questions:

Do all stories include action scenes? What kind of stories or genres often include action scenes? Are action scenes sometimes gratuitous? Can you think of any action scenes that weren't necessary to the story? Why do these attract audiences? When is an action scene effective, and what can you, as an author, do to make sure your action scenes flow smoothly and are easy for readers to follow and visualize?

51

Dialogue

Dialogue is one of the most compelling elements of any narrative. It can be used to advance the plot, establish relationships between the characters, reveal key information about the characters, describe the setting, and set the theme.

It can't be said enough that readers connect with a story through its characters, so it makes sense that dialogue often makes up some of the most critical parts of a story. We humans are, after all, social creatures, and we all experience the highs and lows, the friction and harmony, that relationships bring into our lives. In a story, we see the dynamics of relationships played out through dialogue. And readers connect with those dynamics, especially when they're well executed.

Well-written dialogue flows seamlessly. Readers can hear the characters' voices in their minds. It sounds like a real conversation. However, the secret to good dialogue is that even though it sounds authentic, it's not. If you transcribe a real conversation, it won't work in a story's narrative. It will be peppered with a bunch of unnecessary words and statements ranging from lengthy introductions and farewells, small talk, and *ums*. Good dialogue gets to the heart of matters quickly and efficiently. Consider the following:

"Hey, Joe."

"Hi, Sue."

"How are you?"

"Not bad, how are you?"

"Pretty good. Just waiting for summer so I can take my kids camping."

"I hear you. As soon as the sun comes out, I'm heading to the beach."

"Sounds awesome. Say, I wanted to talk to you about a murder case we worked on a few years ago."

The characters speak over six lines of dialogue before they get to the good stuff. It feels like a long slog. But this is what a real conversation would look like, transcribed to the page. We writers use our storytelling magic to tighten it up into a more riveting conversation:

"Joe, I need to talk to you about the Watershed case."

Joe almost lurched out of his chair. He hadn't heard Sue approaching his desk from behind.

Study:

Record a real conversation, and then transcribe one to three pages of it. Approach this exercise ethically—you are not advised to tape people without their knowledge or consent. As an alternative, simply listen carefully during a conversation— notice the *ums* and *ahs*, the small talk, the filler that we stuff into our real-life dialogue. You can also search online for conversations that have been recorded or transcribed.

Practice:

Write a scene that is composed mostly (if not entirely) of dialogue between two or three characters. The conversation should reveal the following: what a character wants (goals), an inner struggle, a character's strengths, a character's weaknesses, and at least one cue about each character's personality.

Questions:

Why does real human conversation translate poorly to the page? How can dialogue be used to helps readers gain deeper understanding of the characters? Why is dialogue one of the most important elements of storytelling?

52

Distinct Voices

We can learn a lot about characters from how they speak. People from Boston doesn't talk the same way as people from Kentucky, and middle-school kids don't use the same vocabulary as college graduates. Everything from the families we're born into and the communities in which we're raised to our education, career, and personal interests forms the way we speak.

In addition, most people have favorite words and catchphrases that they frequently use. We latch on to certain terms, and they get embedded into our vocabularies. Sometimes we pick up these words because we like them; other times we adopt them because we hear them frequently from our social circles.

We also speak with our own cadence. Rhythm and inflection are often regional, but even within regions—even within your own family—if you really listen to the way people talk, you'll find that each person has a unique way of stringing words together, and they speak with a particular tone and attitude. It's quite possible that if you read a transcription of conversations between your friends and family members with the names of each speaker redacted, you could identify all of them.

Developing unique speaking styles for each character in a story makes them more realistic. We can often tell who is speaking due to the content of their dialogue. Mary's obsessed with science, so if a character is making a reference to physics, it's probably Mary. But good dialogue is distinct, regardless of what's being said, which is why each character needs their own voice.

Study:

Distinct dialogue is often better executed in film and television than in books. Writers don't always make each character's dialogue unique, but because actors speak their dialogue, they bring their own, individual flavor to it. Find a scene from a movie or TV show that depicts a conversation between three or more characters (the more, the better). Transcribe the dialogue from the scene (or find the script to save some time). Study each character's style of speaking, and write a short paragraph analyzing each character's speech patterns. Look for unique words and phrases, cadence, accents or dialects, tone, and attitude.

Practice:

Write a dialogue scene between three or more characters, giving each character a distinct voice. You can use characters from one of your existing projects or create new characters for this exercise. If necessary, spend about five minutes sketching each character's backstory in advance, which will inform their speaking styles. Write a scene that is at least 750 words.

Questions:

If all characters in a story share similar voices, how is the reader's experience hindered? What are some techniques you can use to make each character's voice more distinct? Have you ever read a story and were confused about which character was speaking in a dialogue scene?

53

Exposition

Exposition is everything in a story that isn't action or dialogue. Exposition provides background information and details about the plot, characters, and setting. It includes backstory, information dumps, and other details about the story's events.

The Girl with the Dragon Tattoo is packed with exposition, which provides extensive background information pertaining to the story's plot and characters. It provides readers a deeper understanding of events in the story's past that led to its present circumstances.

Although exposition is less thrilling than action and dialogue, it can be captivating when written well, and it is a useful tool for making sure readers have a better understanding of a story. In most cases, exposition is best kept to a minimum, and background information is ideally revealed through action and dialogue; however, some stories require deeper exploration of the story world, and exposition can be preferable to showing characters sitting around, awkwardly explaining this kind of background information to one another for the readers' benefit.

Study:

Find a story with at least one page of exposition that doesn't include any action or dialogue. Write a critique of the excerpt, answering the following questions: Is the information interesting? Is it essential to the story? Was it easy to visualize?

Did it feel like an information dump, or did it fit seamlessly within the narrative?

Practice:

Write a page of narrative exposition (about 250-350 words) without any action or dialogue. Remember, exposition doesn't include action or dialogue, and it provides background information—ideally this information is essential for the reader to better understand the story's events and characters.

Questions:

Could flashbacks be used in place of exposition when a narrative needs to explain events in a story's past? Why would exposition be preferable to flashbacks, even though flashbacks use action and dialogue whereas exposition does not? When is it better to use action and dialogue to reveal background information, and when is exposition preferable?

54

Description

Description helps readers visualize a story and its characters by providing details about the story world and its inhabitants. Description might be a string of sentences about a character's height, weight, hair color, eye color, and clothing— or it could be a short paragraph depicting a room's furnishing, lighting, and ambiance. Description provides images so the reader can experience the story visually.

Writers sometimes start every scene with lengthy descriptions of the setting, or they introduce each character with a detailed description of the character's appearance. While this can convey the story visually, it can also become dull and repetitive. It's important to strike a balance between providing enough detail upon introducing a character or setting so the reader can visualize it and refraining from lengthy streams of description that can quickly grow trite. Conversely, we can't wait too long to provide important details—if a reader has spent five chapters visualizing a character with brown hair because the hair color was not mentioned and then the narrative states that the character has red hair, it will be jarring.

Novice authors often stuff their stories with description; they want to make sure the reader can visualize every detail, exactly how the author sees it in their head. However, some details are best left to readers' imaginations. Provide a few key details, and let readers fill in the rest. This encourages reader participation in the story, and it enhances the reading experience. The trick is to know how much description to provide, when to provide it, and which details to include.

Study:

Find five paragraphs of description from at least three different stories. You might find some descriptions that are interwoven with action, dialogue, and exposition; however, try to include at least three excerpts that are pure description. Create a list of details that each paragraph of description provides. For example:

Charlotte: brown eyes, long auburn hair, braces on her teeth.

The Jones home: small, cramped, broken windows, stained carpets, smelly.

Next write an assessment of the descriptions you chose— were these details effective? Did they leave anything to the imagination? Was the information important or essential to the overall story? Could the author have included less detail? Should they have included more?

Practice:

Write a hundred-word description of a character. Then write a hundred-word description of a place. Finally, write a hundred-word description of an object.

When you're done, read all three of your descriptions aloud, and assess them. How do they sound? Will readers stay interested? Are the details you included necessary? Do they leave anything to the readers' imaginations? Are the descriptions vivid, and will readers be able to visualize them with ease? Revise and polish to make the prose as compelling as possible.

Questions:

Why are some descriptions intriguing while others are dull and tiresome? What kinds of details are best left to readers' imaginations? In choosing which details to include, what are some best practices you can adopt? What would happen if a story included no description?

55

Weaving It All Together

An experienced author knows how weave action, dialogue, description, and exposition together to form a smooth and seamless narrative.

It's easy to write in blocks: a paragraph of description to set the scene followed by a bit of action and dialogue to show what's happening in the story, and then some exposition to provide context for the characters and the events. Blending these elements makes every moment in the story more vital. For example, if we read a block of text describing a character's appearance, a few details might get lost in the fray, but when one key descriptive detail is revealed via dialogue, it has a better chance of sticking in the reader's mind.

Consider the following description:

> Maya's small frame was topped off with a head of wild, frizzy hair. Her catlike eyes were quick, and she was always smirking. She wore leggings under a loose tunic, with knee-high boots and a tattered velvet scarf draped around her shoulders. She wore no jewelry, and her nails were bitten to the quick.

Now consider revealing one of these details at another point in the story, through dialogue:

> Jones reached across the table and took Maya's hands in his. "You've chewed your nails off," he said, lifting her fingertips to his mouth and gently kissing them.

Either approach works, and the best choice will depend on

the story. Do Maya's bitten nails represent something important, something that will be relevant to her relationship with Jones? Or are they simply part of who she is? Bitten nails could indicate a lifelong habit, or they could have some meaning to the story's events or Maya's character. What if she started biting them after her best friend went missing? What if Jones is a detective trying to find Maya's best friend? The answers to these questions could drive the decision about where to reveal this detail and whether it belongs in a paragraph of pure description or if it should be given more prominence in a dialogue scene.

Study:

Choose a story, and make a copy of an entire chapter. You can take photos of the pages and print them out or use a printer or photocopier. Go through and mark up the text to denote action, dialogue, description, and exposition. You can use different-colored highlighters or underline with different-colored pens. Then write a short analysis about the author's style. Were these elements kept separate, or were they interwoven? Did the author make the best possible choices in weaving together various elements of the narrative?

Practice:

Write a scene of at least a thousand words that includes action, dialogue, description, and exposition. Include one block of each of these elements, plus at least three paragraphs in which these elements are interwoven.

Questions:

What are the benefits and drawbacks of blocking off

narrative elements, such as action, dialogue, description, and exposition? How does interweaving these elements change the reader's experience, or does it? Does the decision to keep the elements separate or interwoven depend on the story?

56

Point of View

Point of view is the perspective from which a story is written. There are three points of view that you'll find in narrative fiction.

First person is usually told from the protagonist's perspective, but the narrator can also be a secondary or even tertiary character in the story. First-person point of view is most easily identified by a narrator who refers to himself or herself as "I." It allows the reader into the narrator's innermost thoughts and feelings and offers an up-close account of the story's events. However, there's a trade-off: readers don't have access to other characters' thoughts and cannot see what other characters are doing unless the narrating character is present.

Second person is rare; the narrator refers to the reader as "you."

Third person is the most common point of view because it offers the most flexibility. The narrator is removed from the story and relays events to the readers by referring to the characters as "he," "she," and "they."

There are variations of third-person point of view:

Subjective point of view allows the narrator to describe

characters' thoughts and feelings using internal dialogue, whereas an objective point of view does not have access to characters' thoughts and feelings; it only offers an external view of them.

A third-person omniscient narrative has full view of the story and characters at all times. The narrator knows everything in the story world but may choose which details to reveal to the reader. A third-person limited narrative only has full knowledge of one character and can only relay events that character is privy to.

Study:

Write a short essay of about 250 words comparing and contrasting first-person point of view and third-person point of view. What are the benefits and drawbacks of each? Do you have a personal preference?

Then find one story written in each of the following points of view: third-person subjective, third-person objective, third-person omniscient, third-person limited. This isn't a test, so if you need help, feel free to search online for titles, but look for titles you've read. For each one, write a short assessment listing the benefits and drawbacks of each type of third-person point of view and how the stories might have been different if the authors had chosen different points of view.

Practice:

Write a short scene (one to three pages) in first-person point of view. Then rewrite the same scene in third-person point of view. Finally, answer the following questions:

- Which point of view worked better and why?

- Did rewriting the scene in third person change the story in any way? If so, what changed?

Questions:

Do you prefer one point of view over the others? Why? Why do you suppose second-person point of view is so rare? What kind of stories work best in first person? Which ones work best in third person? Could both points of view be used in a single story?

57

Viewpoint Characters

Point-of-view (or viewpoint) characters are in focus throughout a story. George R. R. Martin's A Song of Ice and Fire series is written in third-person limited point of view, but each chapter focuses on a different viewpoint character.

When a story shifts between different characters' perspectives, it's critical to make sure readers know at all times which character is in focus. This keeps readers grounded in the story and prevents them from becoming confused.

There are various cues that can be used, such as chapter titles or subtitles. For example, chapter subtitles can state the viewpoint character's name. Details about the setting, a bit of dialogue, or description can also be used to inform the reader which character is in focus.

When stories written in first person shift between different viewpoint characters, it's especially important to make sure cues are present so the reader knows which character is narrating. Giving each character a distinct voice helps readers differentiate between whose perspective they are getting in any given chapter.

If your story includes different character viewpoints, review the first few paragraphs of each chapter or scene that changes point of view to check for cues and make sure the viewpoint character is clear to the readers.

Study:

Find a novel with multiple points of view. It can be written in third or first person. Randomly select five chapters from the book, and then scan the first few paragraphs of each chapter to identify the cues that tell readers which character's perspective is in focus.

Practice:

Write a one-page scene (about 250 words) that includes at least three characters. First write the scene from one character's point of view in first person. Then write it from a different character's perspective in third person. Finally, write the scene so it embodies all characters' points of view (third-person omniscient).

Questions:

Have you ever read a novel with multiple point-of-view characters? Did you get confused about which character was in focus? Do you think multiple viewpoint characters work better in a first-person or third-person narrative?

58

Tense

Stories can be written in past, present, or future tense.

Future tense is rare and looks something like this: *When Jane wakes up, she won't remember what happened. She'll be confused at first, but then she'll get her bearings, take a shower, and go to work as if nothing out of the ordinary had happened.*

Most stories are written in past tense: *Jane woke up groggy and slightly confused. She had no recollection of what had happened, but she took a shower and went to work as if everything were normal.* Past tense adds to the realism of a story because it feels like the narrative is relaying events that already occurred, which is how a true story would be told.

Present tense has gained popularity in recent years: *Jane wakes up and can't remember what's happened. She takes a shower and then goes to work.* Present tense brings immediacy to a story and can feel more immersive to readers.

Present tense works nicely with first person point of view because it gives readers the sense that they are inside the narrator's head as events are unfolding: *I wake up dazed. My head is throbbing, and I have no idea how I got to my apartment or in my bed. I can't even remember where I went last night. I notice the clock and realize I'm late, so I jump in the shower and get ready for work.*

Study:

Find one story written in past tense and one written in

present tense, and then write a comparative analysis. Why does each tense work for each story? Would another tense have worked better? What effect does each tense have on the story and on the reader's experience?

Practice:

Write a short scene of about one page in past tense (feel free to write a longer scene). You can use a scene from a story you've already written or write a new scene for a work in progress. Then rewrite the entire scene in the present tense. Does it change the story? How does the tense affect the energy or quality of the story? If you're feeling bold, rewrite the scene again in future tense.

Questions:

Do you think an author's choice of tense depends on the story, or is it merely the author's style or personal preference? Do some stories work better in past tense while others work better in present tense? What qualities of a story would drive this decision? What kind of story would work well in future tense?

59

Style and Voice

Style is the aesthetic quality of a piece of writing. Rhythm, word choice, imagery, and tone are a few elements that come together to form a writing style.

Voice includes all the elements of style plus whatever makes any author's writing distinct. Think about the way you talk, the way your friends and family talk. You might share similar styles of speaking, but each person also has a unique voice—frequently using particular words, phrases, and expressions—a distinct way of stringing words together and a particular cadence and attitude.

Style and voice are so closely related that sometimes they seem interchangeable. But an author can have a consistent voice even though their style of writing changes, depending on the project.

Study:

Consider your three favorite authors, and for each one, choose three memorable excerpts from their writings. Write a paragraph describing the style of each of the nine excerpts you have chosen. Then group each author's excerpts together, review them as collections, and write a few paragraphs describing each author's voice based on your findings.

Practice:

Make a list of three adjectives that could describe an author's style or voice. Some examples you could use include concise, musical, simple, complex, dark, lofty, etc. Then write a two-page scene that evokes those three adjectives (for example, write a scene in which the language and narrative are musical, dark, and lofty).

Questions:

Can you articulate the difference between style and voice? How would you describe your style of writing? Does it change from project to project? How would you describe your voice? Do you think readers could pick out your distinct writing voice from a list of excerpts from multiple authors?

60

Tone and Mood

Tone and mood give a story a sense of atmosphere—how a story feels—its emotional sensibility.

Atmosphere is often established through a story's setting: An old abandoned Victorian mansion beneath a full moon on a windy night can elicit a dark and creepy atmosphere. However, tone and mood can also come from the characters. A clumsy, awkward character can evoke a humorous tone for a story. And events can shape a story's tone and mood; consider the difference in tone between a story about a star athlete making it to the big leagues versus a story about the effects of war on a combat veteran.

Tone and mood may also be driven by a story's genre. For example, the identifying feature of horror is that it's scary. Romance is romantic. Any genre can be infused with comedy, although there is little humor in a tragedy. An adventure story can be lighthearted or terrifying; a science-fiction story can be thrilling or cerebral; a mystery can be grim or gritty, or both.

One author might use a consistent tone throughout all of their works. Another might use different tones for different projects. And some authors use multiple tones in a single story: A suspenseful scene can follow a funny scene, or a tense scene can follow a sad scene. The tone can even change within a scene: A light or casual moment can turn grave in an instant. A changing tone affects the rhythm of a story, giving it emotional and atmospheric cadence.

Sometimes tone and mood develop naturally from the story's characters, plot, and setting. Other times, tone and mood might be unclear, and it's up to us, as authors, to establish a story's emotional atmosphere.

Study:

Create a simple outline of about five chapters from a novel you've read, and then write a couple of sentences describing the tone throughout these chapters. Then scan through the text, and mark any changes in tone. When you're done, review the story's structure through the lens of tone. What is the overall tone? Can you detect a pattern? How do the tone and mood change as the story builds up to its climax, or do they remain static?

Practice:

Choose two descriptive words for how your story will feel—its tone and mood. Here are a few examples: lighthearted and adventurous, dark and humorous, or mysterious and contemplative. Create a quick sketch for a story, including at least three characters, a setting, and a one-paragraph summary of the plot. Be sure to include details about how the tone and mood will be established. For example, a dark and humorous story might be set in a mortuary with a fumbling, silly protagonist.

Questions:

What effect does tone have on readers? Can tone and mood be used to strengthen a story's characters, plot, or theme? What are some ways authors can communicate a story's tone and mood throughout the narrative? How is tone related to genre, or are they related? What happens when the tone and genre are contrasted (humor within a horror story)? Do you prefer stories with a consistent tone and mood throughout, or do you prefer a story that takes you on an emotional ride, moving through a range of tones and moods?

61

Pacing

Pacing is the rhythm of a story, the underlying drumbeat that gives readers a sense of timing. A story can be fast paced or slow paced. Pacing can change throughout a story, picking up momentum and then slowing down, depending on what's happening. One chapter might span an entire week while another spans an hour. Most stories' pacing accelerates as the climax approaches.

If a story drags in some parts but moves too fast in other parts, then there's a problem with the pacing. It should move along at a comfortable clip that feels natural.

In real life, our sense of time changes. When we're happy and having fun, time moves fast. When we're living in a regular routine, time is slow but steady. And when we're bored, time drags. When pacing in a story changes, it feels realistic, but a change in pacing shouldn't be noticeable or jarring.

Consider a historical novel in which an entire chapter shows a three-day medieval battle, and the next chapter spends just an hour with a primary character who's been injured and is in the hospital. Both chapters might be the same length, but one covers three days while another spans just an hour. Yet the pacing is steady because it's relative: Battles happen fast, and time in a hospital goes by slowly. Pacing doesn't replicate real life, but it should reflect real life and the way time speeds up and slows down in the human experience.

Study:

Conduct a review of a few random chapters from a novel you've read. Make notes about which parts of the story move fast and which move slow. Measure the story's timeline. Is there one chapter that covers an entire year while another spans a single day—yet both chapters are equal in length? Why isn't it jarring to the reader (or is it)?

Practice:

Write two scenes within a single story. You can use a story you're already working on. One should move fast and cover a short amount of time (an hour or a day). Another should move more slowly and cover a longer period of time, like a month or a year. However, try to make both scenes roughly the same word count. Think about what kind of action moves fast and what moves slow. Make sure both scenes are substantial—that is, what happens is important to the plot and characters.

Questions:

How does pacing affect the reader's experience? If the pacing feels off, could it pull the reader out of the story? What happens when the pacing is too slow or too fast? What can you do to review pacing in your work and make sure it flows smoothly?

62

The Unreliable Narrator

In most stories, the narrator tells it like it is—we might not get the whole truth or see the entire picture of what's happening in the story, but the narrator is honest and doesn't misrepresent events.

However, some narrators are not so virtuous.

An unreliable narrator lacks credibility, misleads readers, and cannot be trusted to provide complete or accurate information about the plot and characters. The unreliable narrator could be deceiving readers intentionally or may believe the narrative's own misstatements. Readers might know from the beginning that the narrator cannot be trusted, or readers may not find out until late in the story that the narrative isn't trustworthy.

Famous literary works that use an unreliable narrator include *Lolita*, *The Catcher in the Rye*, and *Fight Club*.

Study:

Find some stories that feature unreliable narrators. Choose

one you've already read. If you can't find one you've already read, narrow your search to short stories so you can read the story quickly and then complete the exercise.

Write a short essay explaining how and why the narrator is unreliable, answering the following questions: Does the narrator lie outright, or do they slightly mislead the reader? Does the narrator believe their own misleading statements? Why is the narrator being inaccurate—to protect themselves or someone else? When does the reader realize the narrator is unreliable? Is the unreliable narrator necessary to the story? How would a reliable narrator change it?

Practice:

Write a short scene of about three pages with an unreliable narrator. Take some time before writing the scene to think about a story situation that will work well with an unreliable narrator.

Questions:

What stories have you read that featured unreliable narrators? Can you think of more than three? What are the benefits of using an unreliable narrator? What are the drawbacks? Do you think an unreliable narrator works better in a first-person or third-person narrative? Why?

Part VII: Literary Devices and Narrative Techniques

63

Allegory

An allegory is a story with a hidden meaning that often imparts a moral lesson. "The Tortoise and the Hare" is an allegory about a tortoise who wins a race against a hare, even though tortoises are slow and hares are fast. The moral of the story? The hare's running speed is useless because he's lazy; the tortoise's slow and steady persistence wins the day.

Allegories are often found in children's tales, but they exist in all forms and genres of storytelling.

Study:

Think of three allegories in the literary canon. Note the title of each, the year it was written, and the hidden meaning or moral lesson that it imparts.

Practice:

Spend about twenty minutes sketching an allegory. Write a summary of your allegory (if you're inclined, go ahead and draft the story), identifying the primary characters, summarizing the plot, and describing the hidden meaning or moral lesson the allegory conveys.

Questions:

How have allegories been used historically in various cultures? Which genres besides children's stories often use allegories? Many of the most well-known allegories are quite old; can you think of any modern works of allegory?

64

Anthropomorphism and Personification

Anthropomorphism is when a nonhuman character behaves like a human. The character could be a plant, an animal, or an object. It could be a robot, a car, or a house. Humanlike behaviors could include talking, walking, emoting, or any other behavior that is not typically seen in the plant, animal, or object that is being anthropomorphized. Anthropomorphism is commonly found in fantasy, science-fiction, and children's stories. The talking furniture and household items in *Beauty and the Beast* are famous examples of anthropomorphism in literature.

Personification is closely related to anthropomorphism. However, instead of a nonhuman character behaving like a human, personification assigns human qualities to nonhuman objects and animals: *That plant is friendly. This computer is tired. My car is throwing a tantrum.*

Study:

Make a list of ten stories (you can include films and TV shows) that use personification or anthropomorphic characters. For each character or object, list at least three humanlike behaviors, traits, or qualities.

Practice:

Warm up with a personification exercise: Write ten sentences that personify various objects.

Then create a sketch for an anthropomorphic character. Describe the character (is it a plant, an animal, or an object?). Give it a name. Note how it came alive (if applicable). Ascribe at least five humanlike behaviors and traits to your character. Finally, write a short scene featuring the anthropomorphic character you've created.

Questions:

Why are anthropomorphic characters appealing to readers? Is there anything a story can do with these characters that can't be done with human characters? In what situations would personification be a useful technique in a piece of writing?

65

Chekhov's Gun and Plot Vouchers

Have you ever read a story that presented an object, character, or scenario that you expected would play an important role, only to discover that it was insignificant, or perhaps forgotten, by the narrative?

Chekhov's Gun is a storytelling principle, which states that elements that appear to be significant to the story must fulfill readers' expectations. If there's a gun in the first act, it must be fired in the second act, otherwise readers will spend the rest of the story waiting for the gun to go off.

A plot voucher (or plot coupon) is a literary device. It's a promise that a story makes to its audience, often in the form of a mystery or question that will be answered or a character or object that will become important later.

Study:

Think of a story you've read in which something seemed important but wasn't, and its presence and lack of later significance left a lingering feeling of dissatisfaction.

Then come up with three examples of stories in which plot vouchers were fulfilled.

Practice:

Sketch an opening scene in which an item stands out just enough that readers expect it to be significant later. Then sketch a scene that will occur later in the story in which the item's significance is fulfilled.

Next sketch a scene in which the narrative raises a question or mystery that will be answered later in the story. This shouldn't be the central plot problem or question. Finally, sketch the follow-up scene in which the question is answered or the mystery is resolved.

Questions:

Why is it important to fulfill unspoken promises that stories make to readers? How can you determine if something in the first act will stand out as significant to readers? Are there circumstances in which a gun might be mentioned in the first act but will never be fired? What if you're describing a person who carries a gun but will never shoot it? What if an old gun is hanging on a wall as part of a room's decor?

66

Comic Relief

A story benefits from moments of humor even if it's not a comedy. A good laugh can break up the intensity of a story, relieve built-up tension, and give it emotional depth.

These jocular moments are considered comic relief because accumulated tension, suspense, or sorrow that readers experience can be melted away with some humor. This allows the reader to reset emotionally and prepare for the tension to start building up again.

Study:

For this exercise, use a film or TV show that you've watched. Choose one that would not be classified as a comedy—the more intense and dramatic, the better. Genres such as mystery, suspense, or tragedy will be ideal. You may be able to list a few moments of comic relief off the top of your head. If not, rewatch the film (or an episode of the television show), and make a list of every moment of comic relief, noting how it fits into the greater drama. What are the emotional tones of the scenes immediately before and after the comic relief? Is the comic relief an entire scene or a moment within a scene? Is it effective at relieving tension within the story, refreshing the audience for whatever comes next?

Practice:

Set up a premise for an intense and dramatic story, and then sketch out ideas for inserting comic relief at key moments.

Questions:

Why does mixing humor into an otherwise dramatic story give it emotional depth as opposed to a story with a single, consistent emotional tone? Does comic relief stand out to you when you're reading a novel or watching a film? Have you ever noticed the effect it has on you emotionally? Do you find it difficult to write comic relief into your stories, or does it come naturally? Have you ever intentionally written moments of humor into a dramatic story?

67

Deathtrap and Deus Ex Machina

If you've ever read a story in which characters are rescued from a dire situation in a way that is truly unbelievable, you've probably experienced deus ex machina. Deus ex machina is a literary device that is best avoided, if possible. It occurs when a difficult or impossible situation is resolved through unlikely or unbelievable methods, often through supernatural intervention.

In many cases, deus ex machina occurs when there's another literary device in play—the deathtrap. A deathtrap is a storytelling device in which the antagonist has captured the protagonist (or other primary characters), and there appears to be no way out. Deus ex machina is sometimes used to resolve a deathtrap.

We love to see characters get out of tight spots, but if the audience is pulled out the story because they cannot suspend their disbelief, then the story isn't doing its job. And deus ex machina, being unlikely and unbelievable by definition, runs a risk of pulling readers out of a story.

But deus ex machina has been around for a long time, and sometimes it's used effectively. If you choose to incorporate it in your stories, give it the eyeroll test—have some friends review the scene, and see if they roll their eyes at it.

You can also resolve problems caused by deus ex machina with a little revision. If you've used deus ex machina to get characters out of a situation, you can always revise other parts of the story to make it more believable. For example, if a character is dangling off the edge of a cliff and a dragon appears and rescues the character, it's deus ex machina. But if the dragon is introduced earlier, the narrative is more believable when it appears at a dire and pivotal moment.

Study:

Find a story that uses deus ex machina to rescue characters from a deathtrap. Brainstorm some solutions that would have been more believable to get the characters out of the sticky situation. Try to come up with at least five alternatives.

Practice:

Write a scene in which it appears the protagonist is stuck in a terrible situation with no way out. It doesn't have to be a deathtrap—just an impossible situation. Then find an unlikely or unbelievable way for the character to get out of the situation via deus ex machina and another that is realistic and believable and therefore not deus ex machina.

Questions:

What happens when you write your characters into a difficult and dangerous situation and can't think of a way to get them out? Have you ever used deus ex machina in one of your stories? What about a deathtrap? Why is deus ex machina often ineffective or even detrimental to a story?

68

Distancing Effect

A distancing effect is a literary device in which a character is intentionally crafted to be unsympathetic, usually so the audience will approach the character with scrutiny or cynicism. It can be used to lay the groundwork for a future surprise (a character that seems nefarious does a good deed), or it can be used to make the audience believe the character is an antagonist, although the character will turn out to be sympathetic or even helpful to the protagonist's cause.

Study:

Think of at least one story in which a character is introduced with a distancing effect. Write a short essay describing how the distancing effect was executed in the story and how the character ended up playing a different role in the story than the audience originally expected.

Practice:

Create a character sketch, outlining some basic traits for a character. Then write a short synopsis describing how a distancing effect for this character would be executed in a story.

Questions:

In what kinds of story situations would a distancing effect be useful? How does planting a distancing effect early in a story make the story more interesting later?

69

Dramatic Visualization

Some narratives include an abundance of visual detail or descriptive action (such as gestures and facial expressions) to make the narrative easier for readers to visualize. This is called dramatic visualization.

Dramatic visualization can help or hinder a story. If it's overdone, readers might get bored of all the descriptive detail and long for more action and dialogue; they want the story to move forward. But when it's well crafted, dramatic visualization can make a story come alive in the reader's mind.

Imagine a character named Ruth who is pacing during a dialogue scene. The narrative might mention Ruth's pacing just once or twice. First we learn Ruth paces as she speaks to Tommy. Later in the scene, we learn that she continues to pace. Therefore we understand that she's pacing throughout.

Another approach would be to describe the pacing throughout the scene. Every time Ruth speaks, her pacing is described. She walks across the room. She turns around. She walks back to the other side of the room. Then she does it again.

If the narrative only mentions the pacing once in a lengthy dialogue scene, the reader might quickly forget that the character is pacing, so the visual of the pacing fades. On the other hand, if the pacing is mentioned too frequently, it can become dull and repetitive.

The best dramatic visualization strikes the right balance, including the most important details and the ideal amount of description.

Study:

Think of a scene from a film or TV show that stood out to you. Translate the scene to prose narrative by writing at least two pages (about five hundred words) describing it. You're adapting the filmed material to prose, so don't simply describe what happened on-screen; turn it into a compelling story, including as much of the dramatic visualization as you can pull from what you saw. In other words, examine what's happening on the screen, and describe it in detail, focusing on things like facial expressions and actions that are not essential to the plot.

Then go through your piece and edit it, streamlining the dramatic visualization to reveal the best details and the ideal amount of description.

Practice:

Write a scene of about a thousand words using detailed description of the following elements: setting, gestures, facial expressions, dialogue, and action. You'll need to use a lot of adjectives and adverbs for this exercise. When you're done, read it back to yourself. Does the language you used cause the scene to come alive in your imagination? Is the description overdone? Give it to a friend, and ask them to tell you what they visualize when they read it. Is there too much dramatic visualization or not enough? Revise and polish as needed.

Questions:

Why is dramatic visualization important in written narratives? How might readers respond when there's too much or not enough dramatic visualization? What if the wrong details are provided? How can an author determine which details and how much description to include?

70

Foreshadowing

Foreshadowing is one of the most common literary devices found in storytelling. It occurs when a scene, event, or character hints at what will happen later in the story. Foreshadowing is difficult to execute because it should feel natural to the story. It shouldn't feel planted, and when it occurs, it should be subtle. Sometimes foreshadowing only becomes obvious during a second reading of a story.

In John Steinbeck's *Of Mice and Men*, Lennie finds a dead mouse and puts it in his pocket, so he can care for it. George mocks Lennie, reminding him that his aunt used to give him mice, but Lennie would always accidentally kill them, even though he was trying to care for them. This foreshadows the climactic event later in the story, in which George kills Lennie, whom he cares for.

Foreshadowing may occur organically as you develop a story, but sometimes you need to intentionally drop hints about what will happen later.

Study:

Find three examples of foreshadowing in literature. Write a short description of each one (at least a hundred words) explaining the moment of foreshadowing, later events that are foreshadowed, and why it's meaningful to the story.

Practice:

Develop a story scenario and how it would be foreshadowed early in the story. You can use a story you're working on or create a new story premise for this exercise.

Questions:

Why is foreshadowing so prominent in stories? What kind of events in a story are best foreshadowed? How can an author include foreshadowing without giving away the future events in a story's plot?

71

Love Triangle

Love triangles are common in all types of stories, especially in the romance genre. But they can also appear in any stories with romantic subplots. A love triangle occurs when three characters have romantic feelings for one another in any combination.

However, there are plenty of twists we can put on a love triangle. Instead of a romantic triangle, there could be a triangle of friendship or loyalty. A group of three best friends might struggle in a friendship triangle if two of the friends are battling for the attention or loyalty of the third.

And it doesn't necessarily have to be a triangle. What if it were a love square, with four players? You can have lots of fun coming up with various geometric relationships among your characters.

Study:

Find a story that includes a traditional love triangle, and assess it. Who are the players? What are the dynamics of all the relationships within the triangle? Is the love triangle the central plot of the story, or is it a subplot? If it's a subplot, what is its relevance to the central plot? How does it play out over the course of the story?

Practice:

Create a love triangle for a story scenario. Your love triangle can be a central plot or a subplot. Write a summary (about 250 words) explaining how it will unfold throughout the story.

As a bonus exercise, try creating a relationship triangle that is not romantic, or create a love square.

Questions:

Why do you suppose love triangles are so compelling, even

outside of the romance genre? Have you seen many love triangles with twists (for example, a friendship square)? What makes a love triangle effective? Why might a love triangle be ineffective in certain stories?

72

The MacGuffin

If the plot of your story is about a character on a quest or pursuing some goal for unknown reasons, you're writing a MacGuffin. The MacGuffin is a plot device common in quests, mysteries, and thrillers. The object of the hero's goal or quest is referred to as the MacGuffin, but the story itself may also be described as a MacGuffin.

MacGuffins are usually subplots, and in some cases, the MacGuffin is not crucial to the central plot.

MacGuffins are common in films and television shows, but they also occur in literature.

Study:

Think of at least one film, one television show, and one novel (or short story) that uses a MacGuffin. For each one, write a brief synopsis of the MacGuffin (about a hundred words each). State the object (the MacGuffin), who's searching for it, why, and how (or whether) it's related to the central plot. If the purpose of the search is unknown to the audience, include a few words about how and why the reason remains unknown until later in the story.

Practice:

Create a MacGuffin for a story. Here are three options to choose from:

1. Create a new story premise that includes a MacGuffin.

2. Describe how you would insert a MacGuffin into an existing work of literature.

3. Explain how you could work a MacGuffin into one of your own stories that is in progress or completed.

Questions:

What does a MacGuffin add to a story in terms of making it compelling or enticing? How might a MacGuffin be used poorly?

73

Paradox

A paradox is any conflict in concept, reason, or logic.

If you traveled back in time and killed your own grandfather before he met your grandmother, would you cease to exist? How can you exist if you've eliminated the source of your own existence? This famous question is called the grandfather paradox.

The predestination paradox says that time travel can't cause changes to the timeline due to predestination. Also called a causal loop, it establishes a time loop in which certain events and outcomes remain unchanged. No matter what you do when you travel to the past, the outcome of the future remains the same.

And then there's the bootstrap paradox, which occurs when something or someone travels back in time and gets locked into an infinite time loop resulting in the object or person having no origin. For example, someone travels back in time and gives someone else a watch. The recipient of the watch ages thirty years, encounters the person who had traveled back in time previously, and gives them the watch. The watch is stuck in an infinite loop, the bootstrap paradox.

Time travel stories often contain brain twisters, somewhat confusing hypotheses about time travel that give some people headaches. Others love to contemplate, discuss, and theorize on the many paradoxes that can occur in time-travel scenarios. But paradoxes aren't exclusive to time travel. Anytime there's a conflict in concept, reason, or logic, paradox is at play.

Paradoxes can get readers thinking in fresh or interesting ways about various concepts. There are plenty of examples in literature. Shakespeare's Hamlet says, "I must be cruel to be kind." There's a conflict in the logic of his statement; therefore it is a paradox.

Study:

Find a paradox in literature (it doesn't have to be a time-travel paradox), and write an essay exploring it. Open with a summary of the paradox. Include a statement about why the paradox is valuable to the reader or why it's necessary to the story. Then examine the paradox. In what way does it defy reason or logic? How can the paradox be explained?

Practice:

Come up with three to five paradoxes of your own. Choose one and sketch an outline for a story that would use the paradox as part of its core plot or theme.

Questions:

Why are paradoxes good thought exercises for readers? What is the allure of a paradox in storytelling? How can an author use paradoxes in their stories?

74

Parody

Parody is a form of satire that ridicules or teases through imitation. Just about anything can be parodied: books, movies, television shows, songs, even people. A parody can be critical or tributary: some parodies make fun of the original in a demeaning way while others honor the original. A parody isn't required to take the same form as the original work: a film can parody a book; a song can parody a play.

Some parodies are loosely based on the original work. For example, *Fifty Shades of Chicken* parodies *Fifty Shades of Grey*, but it's a cookbook, not a novel. Other parodies may follow a plot, theme, or structure similar to the original: *Spaceballs* mocks *Star Wars* and pulls various story elements from it.

Parodies are usually humorous, and iconic works of art are common targets for parody.

Study:

Find a parody of any work of art. A song parody is ideal for this exercise because songs are short and you can quickly listen to them multiple times. Write a short essay comparing the original and the parody. Do they take the same form? Is the structure similar? Do they tackle the same subject matter or themes? What are some significant differences? Does the parody criticize or honor the original?

Practice:

Sketch an idea for a parody of a short story or novel. You can create a parody for a story you didn't like by criticizing it through mockery, or create a parody for a story you liked by honoring it.

Questions:

Do you think parodies appeal more to the fan base of the original work or critics of the original work? Do you enjoy parodies? Why or why not?

75

Reveal

Readers love when a mystery is resolved or an intriguing question is answered. In literary terms, such revelations are called *reveals*.

Curiosity is an intellectual function, but a reveal affects readers emotionally: They want to know who left the anonymous love letter or why the suspect committed the crime. The reveal is like a meal after a long day with no food. But is it a tasty meal or a bland, flavorless one?

Well-structured reveals occur at the right time in the story. They satisfy readers' curiosity, but only after it's been built up for some time. An effective reveal rewards readers by giving them something they've been waiting for. Yet an effective reveal is also believable; it feels natural.

Study:

Make a list of five reveals that occurred in five different stories you've read. Then write a short critique (about a hundred words) of each one. Was the reveal a surprise? Did it solve a mystery or answer a question? How long had the mystery or question been running? Was the reveal satisfying and believable? Was it essential to the main plot?

Practice:

Sketch an outline that leads up to a reveal, or write a scene in which there is a big reveal.

Questions:

Can you think of any storytelling devices other than reveals that stimulate or satisfy readers' curiosity? In what genres are reveals most common?

76

Red Herring

If you've ever enjoyed mystery novel, you've encountered the red herring, a misleading clue that throws characters (and readers) off the trail that leads to the correct suspect. It is most often used in mysteries when a false suspect is presented as a likely culprit but is later revealed to be innocent.

Red herrings can be obvious—if the solution to a problem is too simple or if solving a crime is too easy, the story is probably dropping red herrings to intentionally mislead readers. However, a red herring that's not detectable is most satisfying because the revelation comes as a surprise.

Every mystery includes red herrings. Many suspense and horror stories also contain red herrings, but red herrings can be found in any genre.

Study:

Find a red herring in any story you've read. If you can't think of any, find a short story in the mystery genre; it's almost certain to contain a red herring. Write a one-page analysis of the red herring. How did the red herring mislead the characters in the story? How was the red herring revealed? What was the correct information, or who was the correct suspect? Was the red herring necessary? Did the red herring connect well with the central plot? Did the characters learn anything essential through their experience with the red herring?

Practice:

Sketch a simple mystery concept in which a crime has been committed. Make a list of at least three characters who will be potential suspects. Identify the real suspect, and then choose another as a red herring. Finally, write a one-page summary of how a story would point to the wrong suspect, reveal that this suspect is not guilty, and later lead to the correct suspect.

Questions:

Why do you suppose red herrings are so effective? What's the appeal? Does every mystery need a red herring, or is it optional? If you read mysteries, have you ever read one without a red herring? What differentiates weak, ineffective red herrings from strong, compelling ones? Can you think of any red herrings from stories that weren't in the mystery, suspense, or horror genres?

77

Satire

Satire is criticism through humor, often using irony and overstatement.

The Onion is a famous publication that satirizes the news. Articles on *The Onion* lampoon world events by turning them into humorous, overstated, and often ridiculous reports. Its fictional news stories mock the media, culture, and current events.

Jonathan Swift's famous essay "A Modest Proposal"

criticized the British treatment of the Irish by suggesting they cook and eat Irish infants, essentially saying, "We treat them so poorly now, we might as well eat their babies."

Satire most often plays a role in social and political issues. Irony, overstatement, and humor are useful tools for revealing the darkest impulses of a society or for offering different viewpoints. Satire is often used to underscore and expose absurd conditions and ideas.

Study:

"A Modest Proposal" and *The Onion* are both available for free on the internet. Plenty of other satirical works can be found online and in bookstores. Read a few satirical essays, stories, or news pieces, and write a short essay about one piece of satire, noting the underlying message of the piece, the form (article, essay, book, etc.), and your response to it.

Practice:

Find a topic that you would like to address using satire. Write an outline or a summary for a short story that would tackle an idea satirically.

Questions:

Why do you suppose satire is particularly effective when addressing social and political issues? Can you think of other topics that could benefit from satirical treatments?

78

Sensory Detail

Sensory detail appeals to any or all of the five senses: sight, sound, smell, taste, or touch. If you've ever read a story in which the characters were eating, and you could smell or taste the food, or perhaps you had a sudden hankering for whatever the characters were eating, then you know how powerful sensory details can be.

Sensory detail enriches a story by making it visceral. Appealing to readers' senses is an effective technique for making a story come alive in a way that allows the reader to experience it physiologically. However, the sensory details should be relevant to the plot and characters, not placed in the narrative purely for effect.

Study:

Find ten instances of sensory detail in a novel you've read. Evaluate each sensory detail. Which senses did it engage? What techniques were used to engage the senses? How did it enhance or contribute to the story? Was it effective? Can you think of any way to improve upon how the sensory details were presented?

Practice:

Find an image (a photograph or painting) that depicts a detailed and vivid scene. It could be a romantic image, a haunted house, or a police precinct—anything that appeals to your imagination. Examine the image you've chosen, and write a list of sensory details, describing it. Start by describing the visuals, and then delve into how it would affect your senses. How does it smell? What sounds are present? If there's food, what does it taste like? What kind of textures are there?

Questions:

What are the benefits of using sensory details in a story? How would you decide which sensory details to include and which to leave out?

79

Symbolism

A symbol is anything that represents something else. In literature, symbolism is used for underscoring motifs and themes, emotional and intellectual stimulation, and to establish tone, mood, or atmosphere.

Harry Potter's scar is a badge of honor, a symbol that represents his special ability to survive. In *As You Like It*, Shakespeare uses a stage to symbolize the world and players to symbolize human beings. In *To Kill a Mockingbird*, the mockingbird symbolizes innocence.

There are many universal symbols that you can use: Mars symbolizes war and warriors; the color white symbolizes innocence or purity; underground locations symbolize the depths of the subconscious or the mythical underworld.

But you need not rely on universal symbols. You can use your own imagination to develop symbols that underscore a theme in a story and enhance other elements of the narrative.

Symbols are often concrete items—objects, places, animals, or people—but they can represent abstract ideas or concepts. Symbols are effective tools for highlighting important aspects of a story, and they often emerge unintentionally as a natural part of the story development process, although some authors may intentionally work symbols into their narratives.

Study:

Review a few stories you've read, and identify at least five symbols that appear in them. Make a note of each symbol, which story it's from, what it represents, its meaning within the story, and its relationship to the story's theme and central plot.

Practice:

You can use a story you're already working on or sketch a new story concept for this exercise. Identify the central plot and at least two subplots as well as the main cast of characters in a brief story summary. Then make a list of three to five symbols that could be used to highlight the meaning of the story.

Questions:

Why do you suppose symbolism often emerges naturally, without the author intentionally working symbols into a story? Do symbols strengthen a story even if the reader isn't consciously aware of the symbolism or its meaning? Have you ever written a story only to later realize how symbols were used in it? Have you ever placed symbolism in your stories intentionally?

80

Ticking-Clock Scenario

We've all read a story where characters are working against the clock: A bomb is going to go off, a victim is going to die, the train is going to leave the station. They have a few hours to save the day, then a few minutes, until finally, they disarm the bomb, save the victim, or stop the train — with just seconds to spare.

This is called a ticking-clock scenario, and when it's executed well, it heightens the suspense and tension in a story.

Novels, films, and television shows are full of ticking-clock scenarios. If you enjoy genres like action, mystery, or suspense, then you've probably encountered a lot of ticking clocks. But hard deadlines appear in every genre.

Some ticking clocks feel contrived, as if they've been placed in a story for the sole purpose of heightening the tension. These might pass with the average audience, but experienced critics will spot them. The best ticking-clock scenarios feel natural to the plot.

Study:

Think of two ticking-clock scenarios you've seen in stories—find one that was ineffective or contrived and one that was effective and compelling. Write a few paragraphs comparing and contrasting them. What made one ticking clock interesting while the other felt forced, tedious, or stale?

Practice:

Develop a list of ten simple ideas that involve ticking-clock scenarios, but don't use a bomb, which is the most common plot point that we see in these situations. Try to come up with scenarios that would work across a range of genres (humor, romance, and children's stories aren't obvious candidates for ticking clocks). Remember that any hard deadline functions as a ticking clock (a company is closing, a lover is terminally ill, a family is moving out of town). Summarize your ticking-clock scenarios in one sentence each.

Questions:

Why does a ticking clock increase levels of tension and suspense for readers? What makes some ticking-clock scenarios riveting while others are ineffective?

81

Time Lapse

Stories don't take readers through every minute of the characters' lives. Scenes jump around in time, and the context lets us know how much time has passed. A morning scene shows characters groggy-eyed and sipping coffee; in the next scene, the moon is out, so we know the story has jumped ahead to nighttime. Signifiers and transitions tell us when each scene is taking place.

Sometimes, rather than jumping from one point in time to another, a story needs to skip through time, letting readers know what happened without going into detail or showing the events that occurred in scenes.

For example, let's say a character graduates from college and starts a new job. The story needs to jump ahead ten years. No events have occurred during those ten years that need to be included in the story as scenes, but readers need to know the character has been climbing the corporate ladder during that time.

A narrative can use a time lapse—exposition that quickly covers what has happened during a span of time:

> *Over the next ten years, Jane made countless sacrifices to achieve her goals. She gave up dating, put her social life on hold, and didn't bother to move out of the studio apartment she'd been renting since her days as an undergraduate. It paid off when she eventually earned herself a spot for consideration as the company's next chief financial officer—the executive position she'd been gunning for since landing an internship with the firm right out of college.*

Time lapses can cover any amount of time; they're slightly different from time jumps because they tell us what happened rather than simply moving to a new point in time.

Study:

Flip through a few novels you've read, find three to five time lapses, and study them. Do they blatantly state how much time has passed? Is the time lapse short (a few days) or long (years)? How much information is revealed about what happened during the time lapse? Would the time lapse have worked better if events had been fleshed out in scenes?

Practice:

Write three different time lapses:

- A single-sentence time lapse that spans less than a year.

- A paragraph that uses exposition to span more than one year.

- A lapse that spans at least a decade.

Questions:

When are time lapses necessary? Could some time lapses be avoided? Have you ever found a time lapse to be confusing or unnecessary? What makes a time lapse effective?

82

Flashbacks and Flash Forwards

A flashback jumps back in time and shows a full, fleshed-out scene that occurred before the story's present timeline. Similarly, a flash forward jumps forward in time and shows future events.

Many writers use a variety of storytelling techniques to explain what happened in the past (and in some cases, what will happen in the future). A character can make a reference to a past event via dialogue, or exposition can be used to reveal backstory. However, flashbacks and flash forwards show the events of the past or future in scenes, complete with action and dialogue, as if the narrative had traveled in time.

In time travel stories, the characters move backward and forward through time, taking the narrative with them. Even though they might move back in time a few decades, the timeline of the story remains chronological, through the characters' experience. But a flashback pauses the current timeline to step back in time temporarily, usually to reveal important information from the past that is essential to the story.

Study:

Find a story that includes at least one flashback, and answer the following questions: When does the main timeline take place? When does the flashback take place? How did the events in the flashback relate to the events in the main timeline? Was the flashback essential to the story? How would the narrative be affected if the flashback were removed?

Practice:

Create a premise for a story by summarizing it in a few paragraphs. Then brainstorm a few ideas for flashbacks that would be meaningful in the story. Write a flashback scene of at least two pages that begins in the story's current timeline, then jumps back in time, and then returns to the current timeline.

If you're up to the challenge, try this exercise with a flash forward instead of a flashback.

Questions:

Why might flashbacks or flash forwards be necessary in a story? Have you ever encountered a flashback that was unnecessary or even distracting from the main timeline of the story? What techniques can writers use to smoothly transition into and out of these types of time jumps?

83

Tropes

The classic definition of *trope* is "a figure of speech or the use of figurative language." Recently, *trope* has taken on a new meaning in which it refers to a convention or common motif, often seen in a particular genre of storytelling. For example, danger in the woods is a trope in fairy tales, a love triangle is a trope in romance novels, and interstellar travel is a trope in science fiction.

A trope isn't a requirement in any genre, and in some cases, tropes have been overused to the point of becoming cliché. A ticking-clock scenario in which a bomb is set to go off could be considered a trope and a cliché in action stories because they are common in the genre (trope) and overused (cliché). That doesn't mean a ticking clock or a bomb should never be used, but authors should be aware of tropes that have saturated a genre and only use them when they are necessary to the story or if their story has a fresh take on the trope.

Study:

Choose a genre and think of five tropes common to that genre. Then make a list of three more genres, and think of at least one trope for each. Do the tropes you've identified have specific relevance to the genre (for example, interstellar travel is uniquely relevant to science fiction)? Have any of the tropes become cliché? Why or why not?

Practice:

Write a one-page summary for a story that includes at least three tropes common to the genre in which you're writing plus one trope that is not usually found in that genre.

Questions:

Is it possible to write a story in any genre without including at least a few tropes? Can you think of any tropes that aren't tied to specific genres?

Part VIII: Craft and Process

84

Managing Our Ideas

All the storytelling skills in the world are useless if you don't start with good ideas. Most writers suffer from too many ideas. They give up in the middle of a project to start a different project when they get a tempting new idea. But other writers struggle to find ideas that they want to explore. They think their ideas are boring or unoriginal, or maybe not strong enough to keep their interest for the full duration of a book-length project.

Generating ideas, choosing the best ideas, and seeing ideas through to completion are important skills for a writer to develop.

Most ideas that seem fresh are just old ideas with a new twist. It's almost impossible to find a story that doesn't include various elements from stories that came before. There's nothing wrong with wanting to be original, but if it's preventing you from creating stories, perhaps you're being too hard on yourself and your ideas.

Before diving into a long-term project, make sure you've explored all your options and chosen an idea that you can see through to completion. Before committing to a project, spend some time with its concept and premise. A short story isn't a major commitment, so jump in. But if you plan to write a novel, which could take a year or more, ask yourself whether it's really an idea to which you want to make a long-term commitment.

Study:

You've probably already acquired some story ideas. Maybe they're stuffed in a shoe box, scattered around your office on sticky notes, or stored on your computer or mobile device. Gather up all your ideas and review them.

Practice:

Create a system to manage your story ideas. You could create a folder on your computer that contains one document for each story idea. Maybe you'll use index cards and file them in a box. You could use sticky notes and attach them to pages in a binder, which would allow you to sort, organize, and prioritize. Come up with a system that allows you to quickly and easily store and review the ideas you've had, but also one with space that allows you to further develop your ideas.

Questions:

Why do some writers want their work to be totally original? Why are new ideas so alluring that they entice us away from projects we thought we were committed to? What can we do to make sure we finish projects we've started? Why is it helpful to keep track of our ideas?

85

Brainstorming

Storytellers use brainstorming to develop story ideas: plot, characters, settings, scenes, and more.

Sometimes luck strikes and story ideas flow naturally. We zip through an outline, fly through a draft. Other times, we might have the seed of an idea—an image, a character, or a scene—but we need to expand on it before we can turn it into a viable story concept.

There are many tools that writers can use for brainstorming. Most of us need nothing more than a word processing program or a notebook. Some writers use index cards, which they can later sort and organize into a story. Others use whiteboards. Brainstorming can involve making lists (of scenes, characters, etc.), creating charts, or simply scrawling or doodling ideas on paper.

The tools and methods that work best for you will be whatever helps stimulate your creativity to get ideas flowing.

Study:

For this exercise, go online and find some established brainstorming tools and methods. Make a list of as many brainstorming tools and methods as possible. Then choose at least five tools and methods that you would be willing to try. For example, a tool would be an app for your computer or a whiteboard; a method would be a brainstorming process, like the snowflake method.

Practice:

Choose one of the brainstorming tools or methods that you discovered in the study portion of this exercise. Set a timer for twenty minutes, and use this time to try the brainstorming method that you've chosen.

Questions:

What is the benefit of brainstorming when you're developing a story? Do you think writers brainstorm before drafting a story, or might they sometimes pause in the middle of a draft to brainstorm? Which brainstorming tools and methods have you used, if any? During this exercise, did you discover any new brainstorming tools or methods that you'd like to try?

86

Outlining and Plotting

Planning, plotting, outlining—approaching a project as an architect and drawing up a blueprint—is a popular and effective method of developing a story. Authors who plot their stories ahead of time find that drafting and revisions take less time because they've already worked through potential plot holes, character inconsistencies, and other story problems during the outlining phase.

On the other hand, authors who refrain from planning their stories say they find the writing process more enjoyable because it's filled with surprises and discovery.

Either approach to writing a story is valid, and in fact, most writers fall somewhere in the middle—they do a little planning, a little writing, a little more planning, make some changes, and repeat.

Outlining allows authors to create a concise, bulleted version of a story, which the author can review to identify problems that need to be fixed before the first draft is written. This can save a lot of time during revisions. Imagine placing an important story element in the first chapter only to realize when you get to the end of the draft that it's not going to work. You might have to rewrite the entire manuscript. But if you've worked through the story with an outline, you might only lose a few days of work and a few pages of writing.

There are countless tools you can use to plot a story. One method is to use the three-act structure; another is to use the Hero's Journey. You can make a list of scenes or a list of every significant action that will occur throughout the story. Maybe you will use the snowflake method—starting with a single sentence that summarizes your story, then writing a full paragraph summary, then a one-page summary, and continually expanding the story until it's complete.

There are countless other story structures available, which you can use as plot guides, or you can simply outline your story based on your gut.

Most outlines list the main plot points of a story. Other outlines dig into the details, breaking each plot point into beats. It's up to you to include as much (or as little) detail as you need to realize the vision of your story.

Study:

Choose three of your favorite stories, and craft three different outlines. For the first one, write a three-act summary of the story (setup, conflict, resolution). In the second outline, make a list of the main turning points in the story. Finally, write a one-sentence summary of every scene (shorter works such as children's books, short stories, or novellas will work best for the list of scenes).

Practice:

Create three outlines, but instead of using someone else's story, make up your own. You can write three outlines for the same story or write three outlines for three different stories.

First use the three-act structure to write an outline for a story describing its setup, the central conflict, and the resolution. Write one descriptive paragraph for each of the three acts.

Next write a list of at least twelve major turning points in your story.

Finally, write a list of scenes for your story.

Bonus: Try the snowflake method. Write a single-sentence summary of your story idea. Develop it into a single paragraph. Finally, write a full page. With each expansion, you'll need to add more details.

Questions:

What are the benefits and drawbacks of outlining before drafting a story? Do you like the idea of outlining better than working without a plan? Have you ever written an outline before drafting a story? Did it work for you?

87

Discovery Writing (Pantsing)

Some authors refuse to outline their stories, and many of them say that planning the details of a story takes the fun out of writing it. They prefer to discover the story as it unfolds, while they're drafting. This method is called discovery writing. It's also often called *pantsing*, which comes from the expression "writing by the seat of your pants."

Discovery writing can be fun and messy. We start with an idea—a scene, a character, a situation, even a single image—and then we start writing and see where our imaginations take us. We might make some wrong turns and end up deep in revisions when we get to our later drafts, but storytelling becomes a journey, not a destination. The plot, the characters, the themes—everything develops as we craft scenes on the fly.

Authors often say that with discovery writing, the characters take the wheel and guide the story. A writer with a vague plan for the end of the story finds the characters steering it in some other, completely unexpected direction.

It's a process that can be thrilling and full of surprises and discoveries.

Study:

Set aside about twenty minutes to research authors who use discovery writing. Some search terms you might want to use include "authors who don't outline" or "authors who pants." Look for interviews or articles by authors who have used this method, and then find out why they prefer it. See if any of your favorite authors use discovery writing to craft stories.

Practice:

Set a timer for twenty minutes or give yourself an allotment of five pages (about 250 words per page), and start writing a story. Feel free to take five minutes beforehand to come up with a character, a situation, or a scene to start with. Once you have your starter idea, begin writing, and don't stop until you reach your time or word-count limit. See where the story takes you!

Questions:

Do you prefer writing without a plan, or are you more comfortable with an outline? Do you need some idea of where the story is going to end up, or do you like to leave the ending wide open? What are the benefits and drawbacks of writing without a plan?

88

Drafting

Drafting is the process of getting a story out of your head and onto the page. It's not brainstorming or outlining or planning or editing. It's writing the scenes and chapters of a manuscript in prose, regardless of whether you plotted them out ahead of time. Most authors produce multiple drafts before a story is ready for an editor.

There's no right or wrong way to write a draft. Some authors start at the beginning of a story and work through every scene until they get to the end. Others start in the middle. Some jump around, writing whatever scene or chapter they feel compelled to compose. A few even start at the end and work their way backward.

Some authors write slowly and meticulously; they want to get it right the first time so there are fewer revisions later. They spend more time on each draft but produce fewer drafts. Others write as fast as possible to get all the ideas out of their heads and onto the page. The early drafts are rough, but they are cleaned up later with revisions and fresh drafts.

How you approach drafting will depend on your working style and goals. If you're working under a deadline, you'll probably want to develop a speedy drafting process. If you're writing for pleasure, you might want to take your time and do whatever feels most comfortable.

Study:

Review your last five to ten writing projects. For each one, write a few sentences about how you approached drafting. Did you draft slowly and methodically, or did you draft quickly and without a plan? How many drafts did you complete for each project? Do you approach all projects with the same method of drafting, or did you use different processes for different projects?

Practice:

Choose a drafting method you've never used before, and write a single scene using that method. For example, if you usually write fast and revise later, try drafting a scene slowly, taking your time and trying to get it as tight as possible on the first pass. If you usually write slowly and carefully, try writing fast and see what happens.

Questions:

What is your preferred drafting style? Have you experimented with multiple methods of drafting, or do you always approach drafting the same way? Are there any drafting methods you'd like to try?

89

Revisions

Sometimes we get to the end of an outline or draft only to realize that some of the earlier scenes need to be changed. As we develop a story, new and better ideas often emerge. Maybe a character who wasn't part of our original plan appears. Maybe we think of a new plot twist. Maybe we need to plant more foreshadowing. But we can't do any of that until we've finished the first draft because we don't know the story needs to be changed until we've written it and can see its flaws or areas where improvements could be made.

That's what revisions are for.

Revisions allow us to go back and enhance our work. And revisions aren't just for major changes to the story. Revisions also include editing, proofreading, and other steps we take to polish our words so the text is clean and concise.

Many fledgling authors avoid revisions, and even some experienced writers would prefer to skip them. If you can work with editors, you may be able to redistribute some of the work involved.

The process of revising helps fledgling authors pinpoint their writing weaknesses. If you set aside a draft for a few weeks (or months) and revisit it later, you'll find a bunch of problems that you couldn't see when you originally wrote it, and you'll also see mistakes that you repeatedly make. But this isn't a bad thing. It's an opportunity to identify flaws and work on them.

As critical as revisions are to the storytelling process,

writers—particularly those who tend toward perfectionism or who are attracted to shiny new ideas—must be cautious with regard to getting caught in an endless loop of revising their work. At some point, you have to let it go. The key is knowing when.

Study:

Find an old writing project, preferably something that's over a year old, but a piece that's aged a few months will do. It should be something you didn't polish—maybe the first few chapters of a novel you started or a quick draft of a short story. Review the piece—but don't make any revisions. Just observe what you wrote. Then write about a page describing what you learned from reviewing your work. What mistakes did you make? How could the plot or characters have been better crafted? What would you do differently? How could it be improved?

Practice:

Now take the same piece of writing and revise it. You don't have to revise the whole thing, but try to find at least five pages that you can revise and improve.

Questions:

Why are revisions so important? Why do you suppose young and new authors often avoid them? What revision steps do you employ in your writing process?

90

Research

They say, "Write what you know." But do you really want your stories to be populated with characters that are exactly like you? Do you want every plot to be a reflection of your own life experiences? What if you want to write a story about astronauts, but you're a librarian? What if you want to write historical fiction, but you studied marketing in college?

When you write about characters and experiences that are not your own, you run the risk of making huge mistakes in accuracy. If you write about a scientist, but your knowledge of science is limited, readers who are more knowledgeable than you will be pulled out of the story because you've gotten the details wrong. In addition to damaging the readers' experience, your work might attract negative criticism.

That's why research is an important part of writing fiction.

Authors conduct research to better understand the components of their stories. Research can involve reading an encyclopedia entry about dinosaurs or conducting in-depth interviews with experts and professionals who have the knowledge, experience, and expertise that a story needs in order to be accurate.

So yes, it's best to write what you know. And if you don't possess the knowledge you need, then go out and get it.

Study:

For this exercise, you'll craft three story elements that fall outside of your experience or knowledge.

Create a character: Choose at least three significant traits for the character that you'll need to research. For example, the character might practice a profession you know nothing about, come from a family background different from your own, or be passionate about a hobby outside of your personal interests.

Then choose a setting that you're unfamiliar with. For this exercise, choose a real location somewhere in the world that you've never visited.

Finally, come up with a simple plot or story premise that involves something you've never experienced. For example, if you've never spent much time near the ocean, you could construct a plot about scuba divers getting attacked by sharks.

Conduct research about the elements you've chosen, taking careful notes.

Practice:

Write a summary of your story that's at least two pages (about five hundred words), including elements from your research about the character, plot, and setting.

Questions:

How often do you conduct research for your stories? What resources have you found to be most helpful? Why is it important for storytellers to know what they don't know and research it? Have you ever written a detail into a story only to later find out that you'd gotten it wrong?

91

Process

A typical writing process includes the following steps: brainstorm, outline, research, draft, revise, edit, proof, and publish.

Sounds pretty straightforward, doesn't it? But it's not.

The writing process is a little different for each author, and it's a messy process for most. Some authors don't bother brainstorming or outlining. They're struck by an idea, and they start writing. Some authors write chapter by chapter, editing and polishing as they go instead of completing a draft and then revising the entire manuscript. Some authors work without any notes or research. Others use meticulous note-taking and research.

And many authors spend a good portion of their early careers discovering and refining the process that works best for them. Authors might also use different processes for different projects.

Ultimately each author must figure out what works best for their particular writing goals and working style.

Study:

Find three interviews of authors describing their writing processes. Try to find three authors with different processes. You can use video or written interviews; they should be fairly easy to find online by searching for "author interview writing process." Feel free to include some of your favorite authors' names in your search to see how the authors who have influenced you tackle their writing projects.

Practice:

Think about your own writing process, and write a few paragraphs describing the steps you take to complete a writing project. Then answer the questions below.

Questions:

Do you have a clear, consistent process with identifiable steps? Do you use different processes, depending on the project? Is your writing process effective? Could it be improved? How has it changed over time? How often do you think about your process? What you could do to refine it?

92

Beta Readers

After all the drafts and revisions of a story, you will lose the ability to view your work with a critical eye. You will have become too close to your manuscript to examine it objectively, so you won't be able to see all of its weaknesses and flaws. You also won't be able to see some of its strengths. If you can't see the strengths, you run the risk of editing them out of the story, and if you can't see the weaknesses and flaws, you can't fix them.

Beta readers can help.

Beta readers are a group of people who read a draft of your

manuscript and provide critical feedback that is intended to help you improve your work before you present it to readers, agents, or editors.

Authors use beta readers at various steps in the writing process. It's never a good idea to hand out sloppy work, so the material you share with beta readers should be somewhat polished, even if it's an extensive outline. You can use one beta reader or ten, but you'll find that each reader catches different types of problems. If you want a range of perspectives, it's best to round up a group of several of beta readers.

You can ask your beta readers for general feedback, but you can also ask pointed questions regarding elements of the story that you suspect need more work. Most beta readers focus on story, but you can also ask them to check for technical mistakes (grammar, spelling, and punctuation). However, beta readers are not a replacement for a professional editor.

Study:

Connect with a writer friend, and ask if they have any projects you can review, especially something that's near completion but needs more work. A short story will be ideal, but you can also use a chapter from a novel (the first chapter will be best for this exercise). Check with your friend to see if they want feedback; if not, you'll keep your findings to yourself—it's not appropriate to give feedback on unpublished works without an invitation.

Review the material, and then put together a document listing the problems you found in the work and recommendations for fixes. It's also a good idea to note the strengths and mention them first. Don't check for grammar, spelling, or punctuation for this exercise; focus on character, plot, setting, and other story elements.

Practice:

Put together a beta-reader plan. First figure out how you'll recruit beta readers. Then determine how you'll communicate with them and send them your material. Will you provide them with specific questions to direct their attention to areas of the story that you feel need more work? Will you ask them to identify problems and provide ideas for fixing them? Will you send them the entire manuscript or one chapter at a time? What will the schedule be? What will you do if any of them drop out and stop responding to your communications? And how will you thank them?

Questions:

Have you ever used beta readers? Was the feedback helpful? Have you ever been a beta reader? Did you work with strangers or friends? Will you recruit beta readers for your next project?

93

Editors

At some point, most authors need to consider whether to hire a professional editor to help them fine-tune a manuscript. It's important to note that other writers, English majors, and language arts teachers are not editors. Editors aren't just good at editing written work—they specialize in it. And there are different types of editors.

Developmental editors are similar to beta readers; they help with storytelling and structure; they often work off outlines and summaries before the first draft of a story is written. Copy editors check for syntax, flow, and various other language issues. Line editors proofread to make sure grammar, spelling, and punctuation are spot-on. Some editors provide all these services while others specialize in certain types of editing.

Traditionally, authors would sell their work to a publishing house, and editors employed by the house would work with the author to perfect the manuscript. But these days, with self-publishing as a viable option and with the publishing market growing more competitive, many authors hire their own editors.

It's also important to know that most manuscripts undergo multiple edits—and not necessarily different types of edits. One manuscript might go through three copyedits. Very few editors can catch every problem in a manuscript, and the more problems there are, the more will remain after an edit. That's why it's important to polish your own work as much as possible before handing it over to an editor.

Finally, as with all things, there is a huge range of rates among editors, and you'll almost always get what you pay for.

Study:

Conduct a search online to find editors who provide services in developmental editing, copyediting, and line editing. Review their bios and credentials. Check to see if they specialize in any form or genre. What are their rates? What is their turnaround time? What do they ask you to provide (some

187

might require the manuscript in a particular file format, for example)?

Practice:

Based on the research you did regarding editors, put together a plan, a budget, and a timeline for getting one of your projects edited. Research editors online and find a few that you'd be interested in working with.

Questions:

Have you ever worked with a professional editor? If so, what was the experience like? Do you think you'll ever need to hire a professional editor?

Part IX: Story Scholarship

94

Critiques and Feedback

Critiques and feedback are essential for any writer's development. Whether you're working with beta readers, a professional editor, or a peer group in a creative writing workshop, critiques and feedback can provide the perspective you need to take any project to the next level.

Accepting criticism isn't always easy. It's never fun to hear that your characters are uninteresting or that your plot is full of holes. But we all start somewhere; learning how to accept our failures and weaknesses is the only way we can grow and succeed, especially by using constructive criticism to revise and reform our work to make it better.

There's an art to providing well-constructed and thoughtful criticism that helps a writer improve the work, and the process of critiquing other writers' work thoughtfully and intelligently will strengthen your own writing. As you gain experience critiquing other writers' material, you'll get better at separating yourself from your own work, so you can critique it objectively and then improve it.

When critiquing stories, you should examine every element, from plot and characters to the narrative and literary devices. Use the list below as a general guide:

- **Characters:** Assess the characterization (how a character is portrayed) and the character arcs (or lack thereof) as well as the relationships between the characters. Does each character have a vital purpose to the story? Are the characters engaging?

- **Plot:** Check for plot holes and contradictions, believability (even when suspension of disbelief is required), and flow of major events within the narrative. Are all subplots relevant to the central plot?

- **Setting:** Is it clear when and where every scene takes place? Is the story world believable and easy to visualize?

- **Theme:** Identify the motifs and themes. How do the plot and characters support the themes? How do the motifs and themes underscore the central story idea?

- **Scenes and sequences:** Is every scene essential to the central plot? Do the transitions between scenes flow smoothly?

- **Action and dialogue:** Are the actions within the narrative clear and easy to visualize? Does the dialogue represent the respective characters accurately and distinctly? Do action and dialogue work together to move the story forward in a meaningful way?

- **Narrative:** Are the tense and perspective consistent and a good match for the story that the narrative is telling? Is the language clear, and does it flow well? Is there too much or too little description and exposition? Is the description clear? Does the pacing work?

- **Literary devices:** Identify the literary devices in the story. Do they help or harm the narrative?

- Finally, look for patterns in the story's strengths and weaknesses. Is there a problem with one character's depiction, or is characterization a recurring issue throughout the story? Recurring problems with a particular story element can signal an area where the project needs special attention.

Study:

Choose a novel or short story that you've read. Scan through the story, and mark it up or take notes, highlighting strengths and problem areas. Feel free to make a list of your findings that you can use as an outline before drafting your critique. Then write a critique of the story, describing its overall strengths and weaknesses. Start with the strengths. When you address the weaknesses, be specific and give examples. If you say, "The characterization is inconsistent," provide examples that show how and when the characterization is inconsistent. The length of your critique will depend on your findings; aim for about three pages or 750 words for a critique of a novel-length work.

Practice:

Using the guidelines above, write a critique of one of your own completed stories. Try to be objective; disconnect yourself from any emotional attachments to the work as you evaluate its strengths and weaknesses.

Let your critique sit for a few days, and then come back to your story and devise a plan to make improvements based on your findings.

Questions:

Have you ever provided critiques or feedback to other writers? What did you learn from the experience? Have you ever received a critique or feedback on a piece of your writing? Were you able to accept constructive criticism and use it to improve your work?

95

Studying Authors and Their Works

In literature courses, students are required to go beyond reading works of literature and analyzing them. Supporting reading materials are often assigned alongside poems, short stories, essays, and novels. These materials include historical accounts of the era in which the work was written and the author's biography; sometimes other works (or excerpts) by the author are also provided as recommended reading.

Understanding an author's interests, views, and life experiences often lends deeper insight into the works they've produced. You will read George R.R. Martin's series, A Song of Ice and Fire, with a slightly different perspective after you've learned that Martin is a history buff.

It's difficult to truly understand stories of the past without comprehending the context in which they were written. Modern readers often find *Huckleberry Finn* shocking, even offensive. But knowledge about Mark Twain (Samuel Clemens), his background, his beliefs, and most importantly, the state of society at the time when he was composing his masterpieces clarifies his work and places it in its proper context.

Study:

Choose a story you've read, ideally a novel that was written at least twenty years ago. Read the author's biography (a bio on the author's website or on Wikipedia will do). Then spend some time researching the history at the time and place the story was written.

Practice:

Write an essay of at least five hundred words drawing connections between your newfound knowledge about the author and the circumstances under which the work was written. Does your new knowledge change your perspective of the story? Does it enhance its meaning or deepen your understanding of the work? How did the time and place in which the story was written influence the author, or did it? What can you glean from the author's biography to help you better understand the work? Did you find any information about what inspired the story or what the author hoped to convey in terms of themes and symbolism?

Questions:

How does studying an author's biography lead to a deeper understanding of their work? Why is it important to know enough about history to understand the context in which a story was written? When you read stories, how often do you look further into the author's influences, and have you found this additional research helpful?

96

Plot Analysis

Some readers think analyzing a plot takes the fun out of reading a story. They believe that if you reveal the inner workings and structure of a story, some of the magic and mystery will fade away.

On the other hand, revealing the bones of a plot can inspire greater awe for the art of storytelling and can be educational and informative for aspiring storytellers.

Consider professionals like watchmakers or computer engineers or surgeons. Before they fix watches, build computers, or heal patients, they study the inner workings of their subjects. Watchmakers dissemble watches and study their parts. Computer engineers take computers apart see how they are put together. Surgeons perform dissections in order to fully understand physiology.

Storytellers benefit from doing the same.

When you dissect and analyze a plot, you can see how and why it works. You can see strengths and weaknesses in the construction. This newfound knowledge will inform your work, imparting the skills you need to tell better stories.

Study:

Choose a story you've read, and conduct an analysis using the following guide:

1. Write a summary of the central plot in 250 words or fewer.

2. Break the story into three acts, using a single sentence each to describe the setup, conflict, and resolution. Note the inciting incident.

3. Create an outline, listing all important actions within the story that move the plot (and subplots) forward. If you're working with a long-form story, such as a novel, outline the first few chapters. Does the outline reveal new insights into the story? Can you see how the plot is structured?

4. How are the characters or the story world different at the end? What has changed?

5. What does this story mean? Identify the motifs and themes.

6. Write a logline for the story.

7. Write a critique of the story, identifying what objectively worked or didn't work, and include commentary about your subjective response— what you liked and didn't like.

Practice:

Now analyze one of your own stories. Use the seven questions above to evaluate a story you've written, and then based on your findings, write a page or two describing what you learned and how your story could be improved.

Questions:

Do you think analyzing stories is informative, or does it take the magic out of the stories you enjoy? Is it a little of both? How does analyzing stories improve your storytelling skills?

97

Character Analysis

Characterization may be the single most important element of storytelling. The characters move the plot forward through their actions and dialogue. Readers connect emotionally and intellectually with a story by empathizing with, relating to, or even feeling a sense of opposition to the characters. It is often through sympathetic characters that readers come to care about what happens in a story.

Storytellers must understand what makes their characters tick. What motivates them? What do they want or need? What challenges are they facing? What choices are they forced to make? What are their failures and successes? What makes them interesting? Why should readers care about them?

Only through the act of studying and analyzing characters can we truly understand how they function within stories and how to best use them to tell our stories.

Study:

Choose a primary character from a story you've read recently (the best characters for this exercise will be complex). Then answer the following questions about the character you've chosen:

1. What is the character's situation at the beginning of the story, and what changes it (inciting incident)? How is the character's situation different at the end of the story?

2. Outline the character's arc, noting major milestones for the character's transformation.

3. What is the character grappling with internally throughout the story?

4. What conflict is the character facing, externally, throughout the story?

5. What are the character's ethics (or lack thereof)? Virtues and vices? Strengths and weaknesses?

6. What choices does the character make? What are the consequences?

7. What mistakes does the character make? What setbacks do they experience? Where do they succeed?

8. What are the character's key relationships within the story? Who guides the character? Who challenges them? Who provides support? Who stands in their way?

9. How does the character transform internally? Do the character's actions transform the story world?

10. What lessons, messages, or ideas can be garnered from this character?

Practice:

Use the questions above to analyze one of the characters from a story you've written.

Questions:

Do you agree with many writers and readers that characterization is the most important element of storytelling?

If not, what is more important, and why? How can studying characters from various stories help you craft better characters for your stories?

98

Theme Analysis

We might say that a story's theme is its conscience; theme contains a story's underlying ideas. A story about a young couple falling in love during World War II might be a romance novel, but it could contain themes about the horrors of war, or the necessity of war.

But theme isn't always obvious. Readers get the sense that there's more to the story than what's on the surface, and they may even be aware of what's happening just below the surface, but most people will identify the story's plot as what it's about rather than identifying the themes.

That's why it's good practice for storytellers to examine themes in the stories they read and in the stories they write. Often the spotlight is on the plot and characters, so we have to look a little harder to see what a story might be saying.

Study:

Choose three of your favorite stories, including at least one novel and one short story. Including a children's story would also be useful for this exercise. Answer the following questions about each story's theme:

1. What is the central theme of the story?

2. Are there any secondary themes?

3. Is the theme revealed through plot, character, or setting? What techniques does the author employ to convey theme?

4. What motifs support the theme?

5. What symbols are used to underscore the theme?

6. Is the theme overt or subtle?

7. Is the theme personal, social, or universal in nature? Is it meaningful, and if so, to whom?

Practice:

Choose one of your rough drafts that is near completion, and answer the questions above about your story's theme. Then answer the following questions:

1. Is your theme clear, even if it's subtle?

2. How could you strengthen or enhance the theme?

3. Do the themes in this story appear in your other works?

4. Can you identify common or related themes in the stories you write?

Questions:

Why are themes essential in storytelling? What are some common themes that you've seen in stories? What are some rare or unusual themes that you've seen? What themes would you like to explore in your work?

99

Setting Analysis

Readers need to know when and where a story takes place. We convey a story's setting with description and through action and dialogue as the characters interact with and discuss their environment.

But if we provide too much description, readers might become bored and long for the story's plot to move forward. If we don't provide enough detail, readers might struggle to visualize or understand the story. We must provide enough information about the setting so that readers can visualize it, but not so much that they lose interest or can't engage their imaginations.

A setting might directly affect the characters' experiences. It can contribute to the story's tone and mood. It includes props, objects that the characters use and interact with. Some settings function as characters within a story because they have vivid personalities.

Authors can use a variety of tools and techniques to render a setting, from researching real locations and using them in stories to physically traveling to scout locations or even creating settings from their imaginations.

Study:

Choose a story you've read with a clear and vivid setting. It should be a setting that came alive in your mind as you read the story, a setting you found memorable. Then choose a story with a setting that was vague, difficult to imagine, or inconsequential to the story. Write a two-page essay of about five hundred words comparing and contrasting the authors' techniques for rendering their settings. Include answers to the following questions in your analysis:

1. Approximately how many settings (time and place) were included in the story?

2. How much description did the narrative use to convey the settings? Was the description engaging or dull? Was it vivid or unclear?

3. How often was setting revealed through action or dialogue? How often was it revealed through exposition?

4. Were transitions between settings smooth and clear, or were they jarring and confusing?

Practice:

Now evaluate the setting in one of your own stories by answering the questions above. Then write a list of actions you can take to improve the way you conveyed the setting in your story.

Questions:

Do you think it's easier to create a setting from imagination, as is often the case in science fiction and fantasy, or is it easier to base a setting on a real location? Which techniques for establishing setting do you think are most effective? Which aspect of setting do you struggle with the most?

100

Story Analysis

Conducting a full analysis of a story is an excellent way to better understand the nuts and bolts of storytelling. It's an exercise that will reveal what works, what doesn't, and why. While it's useful to analyze isolated components of a story, such as plot, characters, setting, and theme, a fuller understanding can only be reached through viewing all of the story components collectively.

Study:

Choose a novel you've read, and complete the following:

1. Describe the story's concept and premise.

2. Describe the story's three-act structure, writing a single sentence for each act (setup, conflict, resolution).

3. Write a synopsis of the central plot. Be sure to include the setup, conflict, and resolution. Note all subplots within the story and how they are related to the central plot.

4. List the main characters. Identify each character's function in the story by noting their goal, internal struggle, external conflict, strengths, weaknesses, and path of transformation (character arc).

5. Describe the most important relationships (including antagonistic) in the story.

6. Identify the themes, motifs, and symbols. Describe the thematic patterning.

7. Briefly describe the setting (time and place), and note whether the setting directly affects or drives the plot or characters. Include various settings throughout the story and notes about how the narrative transitions between settings.

8. What point of view and tense does the narrative use?

9. Evaluate the use of dialogue in the story. Is it extensive? Does each character have a distinct voice?

10. Which storytelling devices are used in the story?

11. Identify any archetypes or story beats from the Hero's Journey.

12. Write a logline for the story of no more than two sentences.

Practice:

Use the analysis questionnaire above to evaluate one of your own stories.

Questions:

What can you learn from conducting a story analysis? Do you think it's best for authors to avoid overanalyzing stories, or do these analyses give authors greater insight into the nuts and bolts of storytelling?

Your Journey in Storytelling

As you continue your journey in storytelling, you'll find tools and techniques to add to your toolbox. In time, you'll learn which tools and techniques work best with your writing style. You'll find that some storytelling concepts will serve you well with one story but won't be applicable to another. As long as you continue to study the craft and maintain a regular writing practice, you'll gain experience and expertise. Every project will bring you a step closer to mastering the art of storytelling. Give yourself space to learn, study, experiment, and practice.

There are many ways to learn—you can study short stories, novels, films, and television shows; read books on the craft of writing and storytelling; and seek out interviews and podcasts featuring experienced authors and professionals in the publishing industry.

You'll encounter many advisors who claim that a particular method, regimen, or formula is necessary for a story to be successful. While there are best practices in storytelling that you would be wise to heed, some of the greatest stories have come from authors who were willing to take risks and break the rules of conventional wisdom. Beta readers and editors can help you see your story objectively so you can determine whether the risks you're taking are beneficial or detrimental to your stories.

Most storytellers enjoy making up stories but struggle through revisions. The work of revising and refining a story can be tedious, frustrating, even maddening. But it is through revision that a rough draft—a messy wellspring of ideas—is honed and polished into a work of art.

Sometimes you'll complete a project only to realize that it's sorely lacking in quality; you might set it aside with the hope that you can revisit it in the future and make improvements, or you might discard it and chalk it up as a learning experience. The stories you never share or publish will enrich your storytelling and writing skills—you'll learn something valuable with each one. That's why it's important to see your projects through to completion; even if you don't feel a story is worthy of publication, you'll maximize your learning by finishing it.

It's not uncommon for laypersons to believe that stories come pouring forth from writers, fully formed, and all we have to do is type them up. But creating stories is hard work. It's rewarding, but it's also grueling at times. Sometimes it feels like you're climbing an infinite mountain rather than trying to tell a compelling and interesting tale. Storytelling is not all fun and games, which is why the most prolific authors have made a commitment to the work. A lot of writers call this "butt in chair," meaning nothing will ever get finished if you don't put your butt in your chair and get your work done. The best way to accomplish this is to establish a regular writing routine— preferably a daily writing regimen. The craft of writing is similar to maintaining your physical fitness: to stay in shape, you must work out regularly.

Other than writing, nothing will improve your work more than reading. Focus on reading within your genre, but read beyond your niche as well. You will absorb language and story, and your writing will benefit immensely. If you don't read, it will show in your work.

Storytelling is an enlightening and rewarding experience whether you're doing it as a hobby or trying to build a career. I hope you'll find the concepts, tools, and techniques in this book useful as you continue your journey. Good luck, and keep writing those stories!

If you'd like to delve deeper into these storytelling concepts, check out the rest of The Storyteller's Toolbox series of books on writing fiction.

Visit writingforward.com to learn more.

Appendix: Worksheets

Character Sketch Worksheet

Character Arc

What does the character want (external goal)?

Why does the character want this?

What is preventing the character from getting what they want?

What are the stakes?

What is the character's internal struggle, and how is it preventing them from getting what they want?

How does the character need to change and grow to get what they want?

Personality

What does the character love?

What does the character fear?

What are the character's strengths?

What are the character's weaknesses?

Describe the character's behavior and attitude.

Describe the character's style and tastes, likes and dislikes.

Physical Description

List the character's age, height, weight, and hair and eye color.

List the character's facial and physical features.

What is the character's ethnicity or heritage?

Background

Education:

Skills:

Occupation:

Interests:

Beliefs (politics/religion):

Significant life events:

Miscellaneous

Does the character fill an archetypal role in the story?

Describe the character's key relationships (friends, family, coworkers, enemies).

Describe the beginning, middle, and end of this character's arc.

Write the character's backstory.

Write a few diary entries in the character's voice.

World-Building Worksheet

Time and Place

Location(s):

Time(s):

Geography

Geographical features:

Climate:

Natural resources:

Society

Demographics:

Social structure (classes):

Production:

Economy:

Government (political structure):

Laws:

Law enforcement and justice system:

Military:

Allies and enemies:

Culture

Language:

Food:

Entertainment, recreation, and leisure:

Art, music, and lore:

Religion:

Customs and rituals:

Festivals and holidays:

Technology and Magic

Technology:

Magic systems:

Summary

Write a one-page summary of the story world.

Backstory

Write about the history and background of the story world, describing major events that shaped its civilization.

Story Structure Worksheets

The following two worksheets are for analyzing or developing stories.

The Three-Act Structure

List the characters and their relationships to one another.

Describe the story world.

Act I: Setup

What is the protagonist's goal and what's holding them back?

Describe the inciting incident, which presents a dramatic and permanent change for the protagonist, raising the central story question or challenge.

What central conflict does the protagonist face?

Act II: Conflict

How does the protagonist attempt to tackle the challenge or solve the problem at the heart of the story? How do these attempts cause the situation to worsen?

Along the way there are successes and failures. What are they?

How do the stakes get higher? How does the tension increase?

What skills or traits does the protagonist need to acquire?

What is the climax, the most intense moment of the story, when conflict, tension, and stakes are at their highest?

Act III: Resolution

How do the central story problem (main plot) and all subplots get resolved?

How has the protagonist (and possibly the other characters) changed from who and where they were in the beginning?

How does the story world change as a result of the events that occurred throughout the story?

The Hero's Journey

Archetypes

- Hero:

- Herald:

- Mentor:

- Threshold Guardian:

- Shadow:

- Shapeshifter:

- Trickster:

- Allies:

Act I: Departure

1. Ordinary World:

2. Call to Adventure:

3. Refusal of the Call:

4. Meeting with the Mentor:

5. Crossing the First Threshold:

Act II: Initiation

6. Tests, Allies, and Enemies:

7. Approach to the Inmost Cave:

8. Ordeal:

9. Reward:

Act III: Return

    10. The Road Back:

    11. Resurrection:

    12. Return with Elixir:

Story Analysis Worksheet

Title:

Author (or Director):

Medium/Form:

Genre:

Concept:

Premise:

Logline:

Characters

Protagonist:

Antagonist:

Other primary characters:

Secondary characters:

Tertiary characters:

Describe the protagonist's external goal and internal struggle.

Describe the protagonist's character arc.

Describe one to three key relationships and how they develop.

Plot

Summarize the plot (core conflict) in fewer than five hundred words.

Identify one to three subplots.

List five to ten narrative techniques used in the story.

Can you identify a structure (three-act structure, Hero's Journey, etc.)? If so, write a brief overview explaining how the story adhered to the structure.

Setting

Describe the story's setting.

Theme

List the motifs and symbols in the story.

What is the central theme of the story?

What other themes appear in the story?

Style and Voice

What is the tense and point of view?

How would you describe the narrative style and voice?

Critical Analysis

Considering the basic building blocks of effective storytelling, how does this story measure up? Describe three strengths and three weaknesses in the storytelling.

Works Cited

Books

Aesop. "The Hare and the Tortoise." In *Aesop's Fables*. New York: Signet Classics, 2004.

Baum, Frank L. *The Wonderful Wizard of Oz*. New York: Signet Classics, 1984.

Booker, Christopher. *The Seven Basic Plots: Why We Tell Stories*. New York: Continuum, 2004.

Campbell, Joseph. *The Hero with a Thousand Faces*. Princeton, NJ: Princeton University Press, 1973.

Collins, Suzanne. The Hunger Games (Trilogy). New York: Scholastic Press, 2008–2010.

Flynn, Gillian. *Gone Girl*. New York: Broadway Books, 2012.

Fowler, F.L. *Fifty Shades of Chicken: A Parody in a Cookbook*. New York: Clarkson Potter, 2012.

Jacob Grimm and Wilhelm Grimm. "Little Red Riding Hood." In *Grimms' Fairy Tales*. London: Macmillan Collector's Library, 2016.

James, E.L. *Fifty Shades of Grey*. New York: Vintage Books, 2011.

James, Henry. *The Turn of the Screw*. New York: Dover Publications Inc. 1991.

Larsson, Stieg. *The Girl with the Dragon Tattoo*. New York: Random House, 2008.

Lee, Harper. *To Kill a Mockingbird*. New York: HarperCollins, 1985.

Martin, George R. R. A Song of Ice and Fire (Series). New York: Bantam Books, 1991–2011.

Nabokov, Vladimir. *Lolita*. New York: Random House,

Inc. 1997.

Palahniuk, Chuck. *Fight Club*. New York: W.W. Norton & Company Inc., 2005.

Rowling, J. K. Harry Potter (Series). New York: Scholastic, 1998–2007.

Salinger, J. D. *The Catcher in the Rye*. New York: Little, Brown, 1951.

Seuss, Dr. *Green Eggs and Ham*. New York: Beginner Books, 1960.

Shakespeare, William. *As You Like It*. New York: Washington Square Press, 2004.

Shakespeare, William. *Hamlet*. New York: Dover Publications, Inc. 2009.

Steinbeck, John. *Of Mice and Men*. New York: Penguin Group (USA) Inc., 1993.

Swift, Jonathan. "A Modest Proposal." In *A Modest Proposal and Other Satirical Works*. Mineola, NY: Dover, 1996.

Tolkien, J. R. R. Lord of the Rings (Trilogy). New York: Ballantine Books, 1975.

Twain, Mark. *The Adventures of Huckleberry Finn*. New York: Bantam Books, 2003.

Vogler, Christopher. *The Writer's Journey: Mythic Structure for Writers*. 3rd ed. Studio City, CA: Michael Wiese Productions, 1998.

Film

Alien. Directed by Ridley Scott. 20th Century Fox, 1979.

Avatar. Directed by James Cameron. 20th Century Fox, 2009.

Beauty and the Beast. Directed by Gary Trousdale and Kirk

Wise. Buena Vista Pictures, 1991.

Dark Knight, The. Directed by Christopher Nolan. Warner Bros. Pictures, 2008.

Few Good Men, A. Directed by Rob Reiner. Columbia Pictures, 1992.

Hidden Figures. Directed by Theodore Melfi. 20th Century Fox, 2016.

Jane Austen Book Club, The. Directed by Robin Swicord. Sony Pictures Classics, 2007.

Jurassic Park. Directed by Steven Spielberg. Universal Pictures, 1993.

Office Space. Directed by Mike Judge. 20th Century Fox, 1999.

Primal Fear. Directed by Gregory Hoblit. Paramount Pictures, 1996.

Pulp Fiction. Directed by Quentin Tarantino. Miramax Films, 1994.

Spaceballs. Directed by Mel Brooks. MGM/UA Communications Co., 1987.

Star Wars: Episode IV: A New Hope. Directed by George Lucas. 20th Century Fox, 1977.

Titanic. Directed by James Cameron. 20th Century Fox, 1997.

Usual Suspects, The. Directed by Bryan Singer. Gramercy Pictures, 1995.

Television

Big Bang Theory, The. Television series created by Chuck Lorre and Bill Prady. CBS, 2007-present.

Sex and the City. Television series created by Darren Star. HBO, 1998–2004.

Star Trek (The Original Series). Television series created by Gene Roddenberry. NBC, 1966–1969.

Other

Onion, The. 2018. https://www.theonion.com.

Keep Writing Stories!

Thank you for reading *Story Drills: Fiction Writing Exercises* from the Storyteller's Toolbox series. If you'd like to be notified when new books on the craft of writing are released, sign up for my newsletter at writingforward.com. As a subscriber, you'll get exclusive offers, creative writing tips and ideas, and other goodies.

If you enjoyed this book and found it beneficial, please consider leaving a review.

Storytelling is an important and meaningful part of human culture. Stories exist to educate, inform, entertain, and share the experiences that connect us all. Stories can change the world.

Keep writing!

About the Author

Melissa Donovan is the founder and editor of Writing Forward, a blog packed with creative writing tips and ideas.

Melissa started writing poetry and song lyrics at age thirteen. Shortly thereafter, she began keeping a journal. She studied at Sonoma State University, earning a BA in English with a concentration in creative writing. Since then, Melissa has worked as an author, copywriter, professional blogger, and writing coach.

Writing Forward

Writing Forward features creative writing tips, ideas, tools, and techniques, as well as writing exercises and prompts that offer inspiration and help build skills.

To get more writing tips and ideas and to receive notifications when new books on the craft of writing are released, visit Writing Forward.

www.writingforward.com

Made in the USA
Lexington, KY
21 March 2019